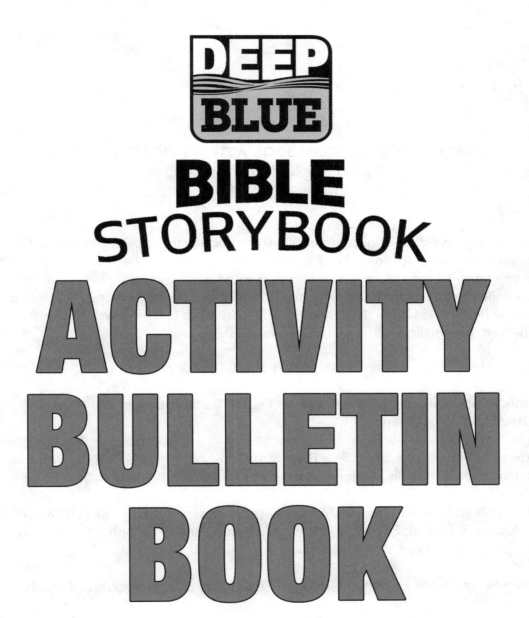

DEEP BLUE

BIBLE STORYBOOK

ACTIVITY BULLETIN BOOK

Abingdon Press

Nashville

Contents

The Earth
Genesis 1:1-19

In the beginning, there was nothing. God said, "Let there be light!" and light was made. God kept speaking and created the sky, water, land, plants, stars, the sun, and the moon! Add the sun.

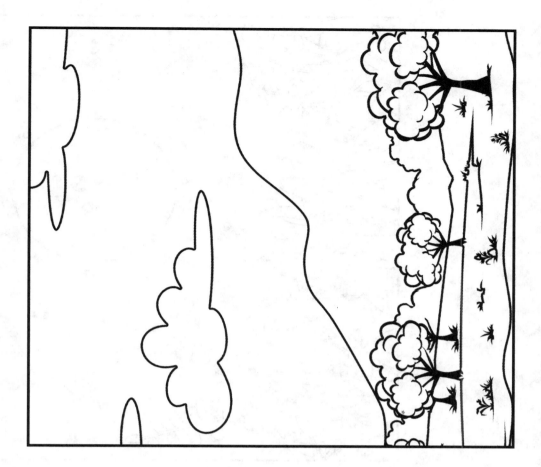

Draw your favorite place on God's earth.

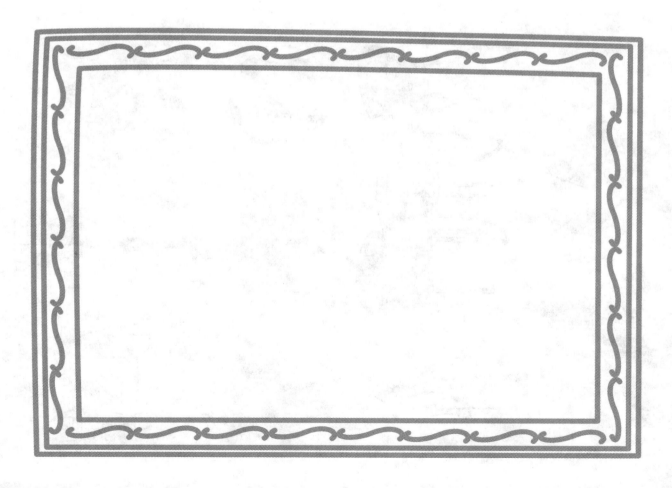

1

Connect the dots to see what God created.

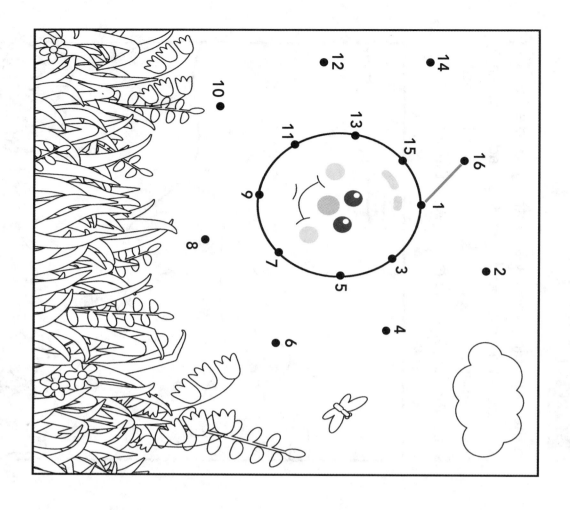

Circle everything that gives light.

DEEP BLUE

Living Things
Genesis 1:20-25

God created animals that live in water, animals that fly in the air, and animals that live on the land. Everything God created was good! Add fish to the picture.

Draw or describe your favorite animal.

Draw lines between the matching birds.

Circle the items that don't belong in the picture below.

In God's Image

Genesis 1:26–2:4

God spoke, "Let there be people," and people were created. The people would take care of everything God had made.

Everything God created is good -- including you! Draw a picture of yourself. God loves you!

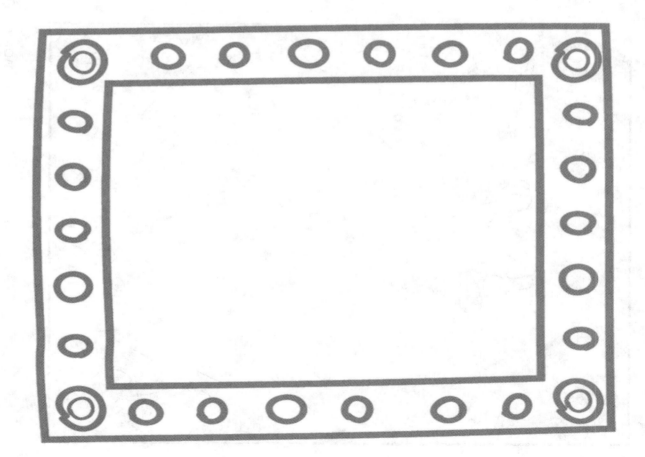

Circle ways that you can care for God's creation.

God was very creative when designing animals and people. Use your imagination to finish the picture below!

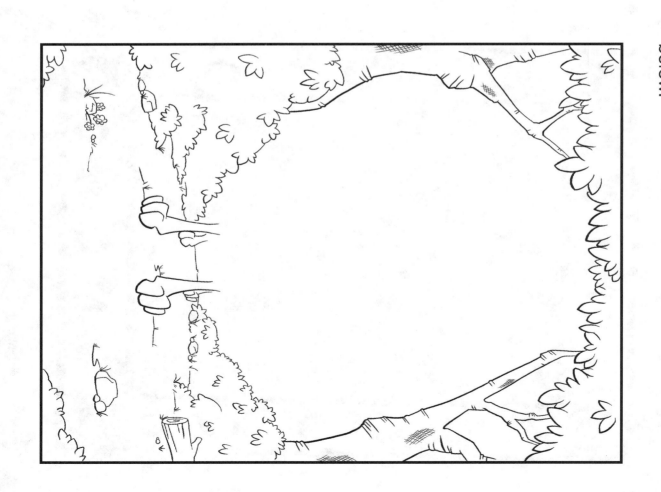

Adam and Eve
Genesis 2:10–3:24

God gave Adam and Eve a beautiful garden. When they disobeyed God, they had to leave the garden and live out in the world.

How do you think Adam and Eve felt in this story before they ate the special fruit? How do you think they felt after? Draw their feelings on the faces below.

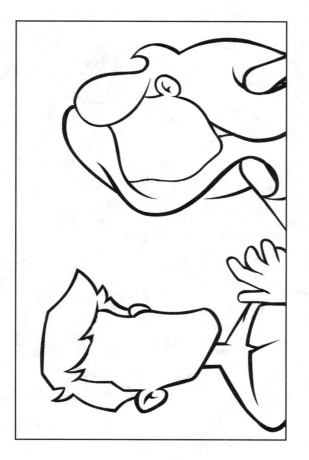

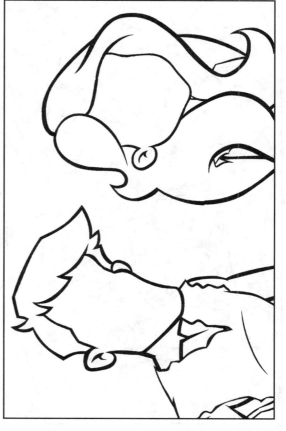

4

Number the scenes in the order they happened.

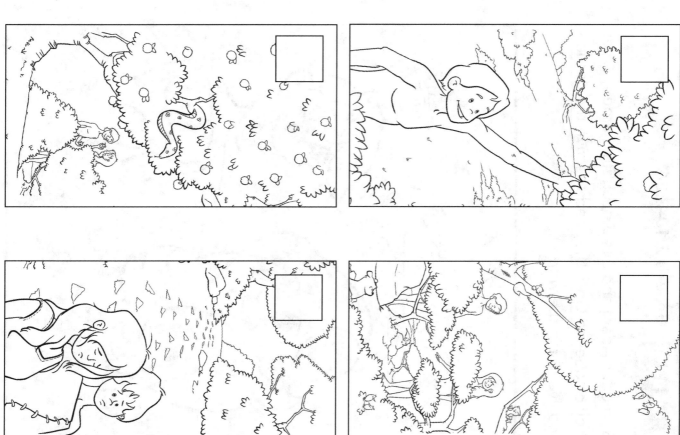

God saw that the man was lonely without a friend.
Help the friends find their way to each other.

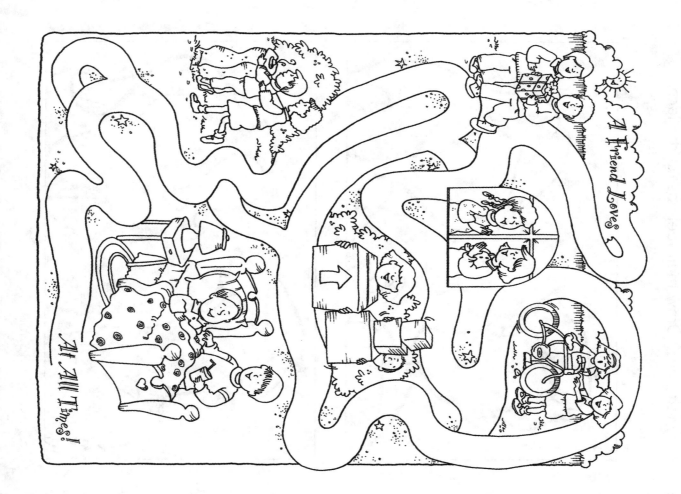

DEEP BLUE

Noah Builds the Ark

Genesis 6:13-22

God told Noah that the world would be flooded. Then God told Noah to build a big wooden boat to keep his family safe. Noah did everything God told him to do.

Noah included places for the animals to sleep and food for them to eat. Prepare this stall for a pair of animals. Then add the animals.

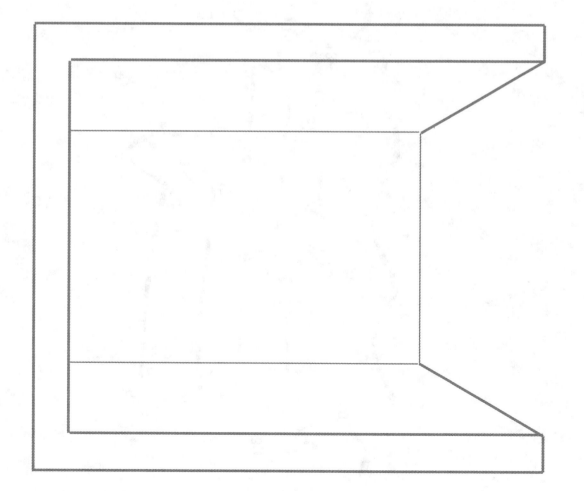

Help Noah and his family find their way to the ark before it starts raining!

Start

End

Connect the dots to see what the ark looked like.

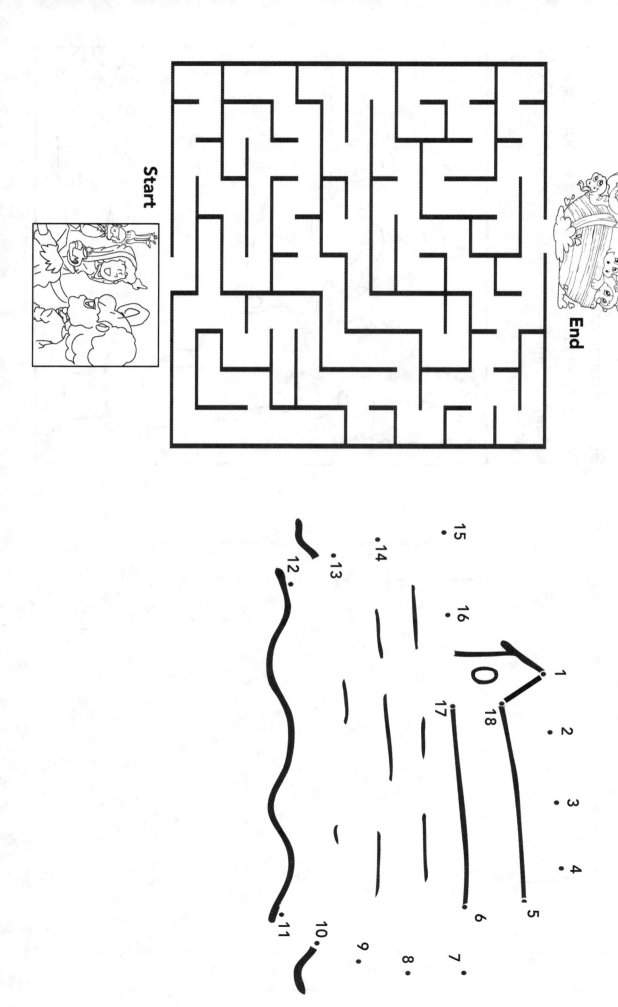

God told Noah to take his family and two of every kind of animal into the ark. It started raining and kept raining for 40 days!

Lots and lots and lots of rain isn't good for creation, but some rain is! Draw a plant that needs rain to grow.

Number the pictures in the order of the story.

DEEP BLUE

Sending Out the Dove
Genesis 8:1-19

When the rain stopped, Noah sent out a dove to search for dry land. When the dove returned with an olive leaf in its beak, Noah knew that the ground was dry and it was okay to get off the ark.

God didn't forget about Noah, his family, and the animals! God will never forget about you, either. Who or what will you always remember?

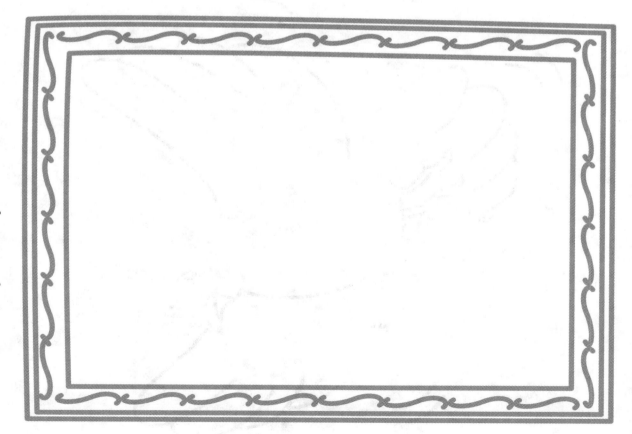

7

Circle the matching doves.

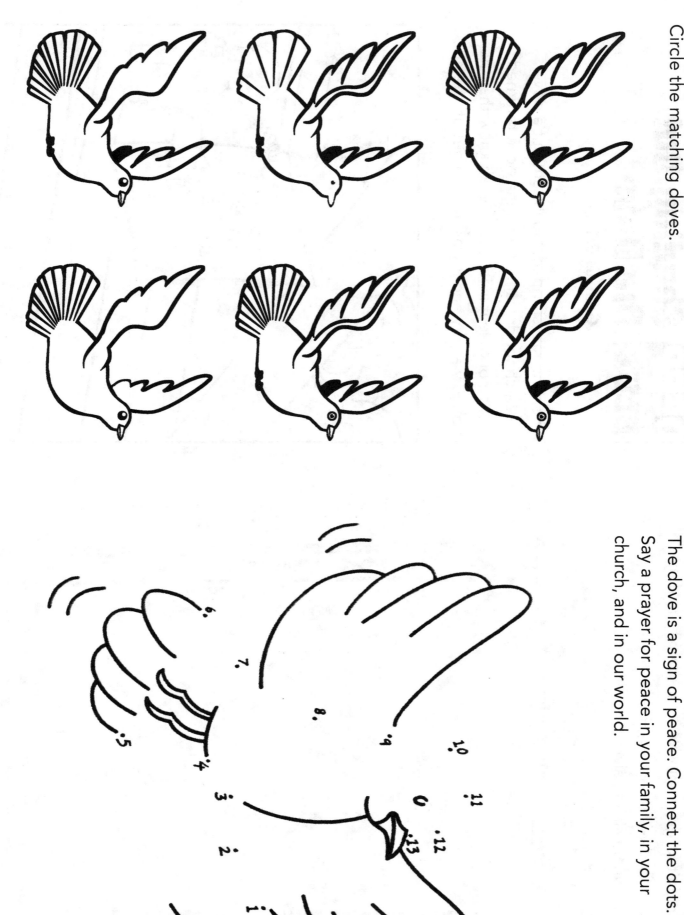

The dove is a sign of peace. Connect the dots. Say a prayer for peace in your family, in your church, and in our world.

The Rainbow Promise

Genesis 8:20–9:17

After the flood, God made a promise never again to hurt the earth. God placed the rainbow in the sky to remind us of the promise.

Rainbows remind us that God will love us forever. Draw or write about someone you will love forever.

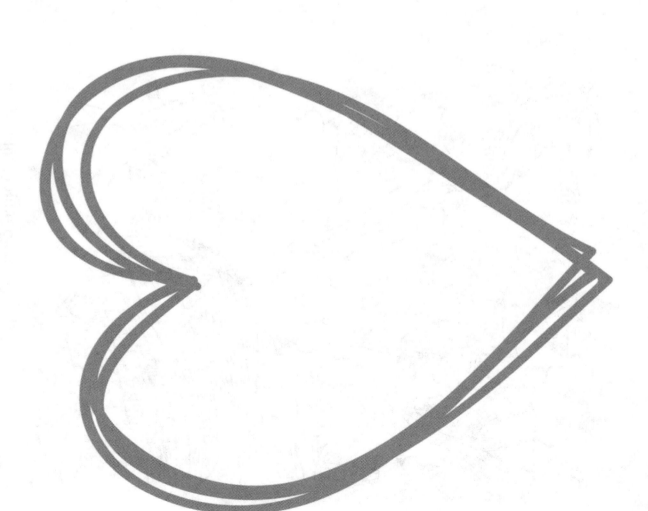

Can you find your way through the rainbow?

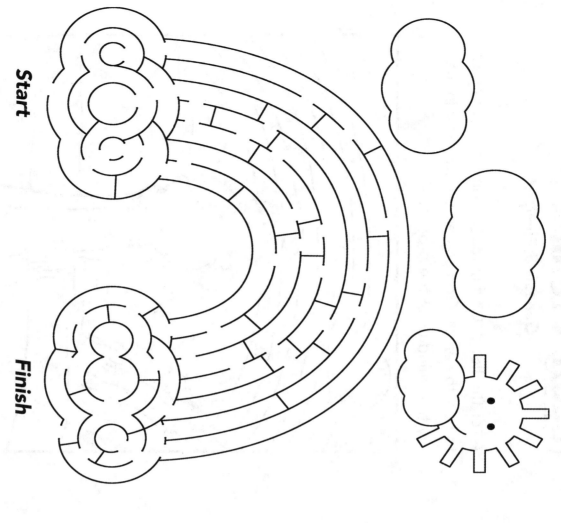

Start

Finish

After the rain dried up, the ark was on solid ground. How many people, birds, and animals can you find in the picture?

Abraham and Sarah

Genesis 12:1-9, 15:1-6

God said to Abraham, "Go where I send you, and I will bless you." Abraham and his wife, Sarah, traveled to a new land, which God gave to them.

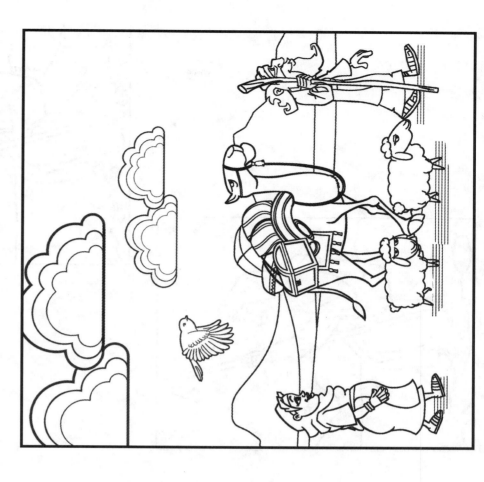

God promised to give Abraham as many children as there are stars in the sky. And God did! We are all part of Abraham's family. Add a star for each member of your family – then add even more!

Circle seven differences between the pictures.

Complete the maze to help Abraham and Sarah find their new home in Canaan.

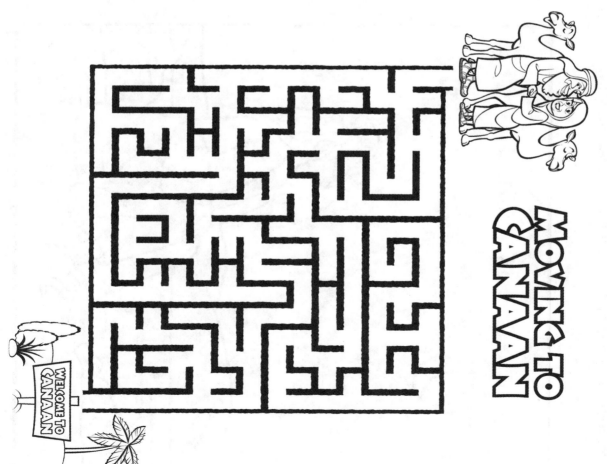

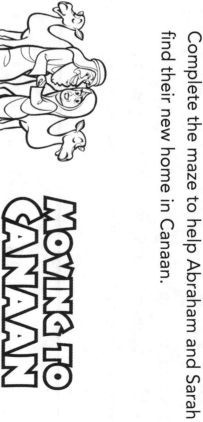

MOVING TO CANAAN

WELCOME TO CANAAN

DEEP BLUE Abraham and Lot
Genesis 13:1-12

Abraham and his nephew, Lot, argued over who would get to live where. Abraham found a way for them to share the land.

Abraham and Lot had a fight. Write or think of kind words they could say to each other.

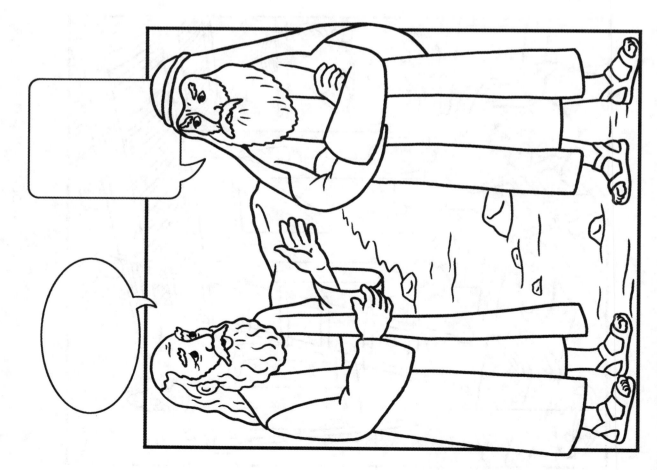

Find the words hidden in the puzzle below.

```
S  H  E  E  P  T  O
A  T  H  F  A  C  R
V  L  N  A  R  I  L
K  O  D  M  G  W  A
V  T  L  V  V  N
S  H  A  R  E  Z  D
A  B  R  A  H  A  M
```

ABRAHAM   LAND
LOT   ARGUE
SHEEP   SHARE

Help Abraham pack by circling the items he would need to take with him to move: sandals, blankets, staff, lamp, food, bag, bedroll.

The Birth of Isaac

Genesis 18:1-15; 21:1-7

Three visitors appeared to Abraham and told him that Sarah would have a baby. Sarah didn't believe it – she was too old to have a baby! But the next year, God gave Sarah and Abraham a baby named Isaac.

Sarah and Abraham were very old when Isaac was born. Draw the oldest person you know.

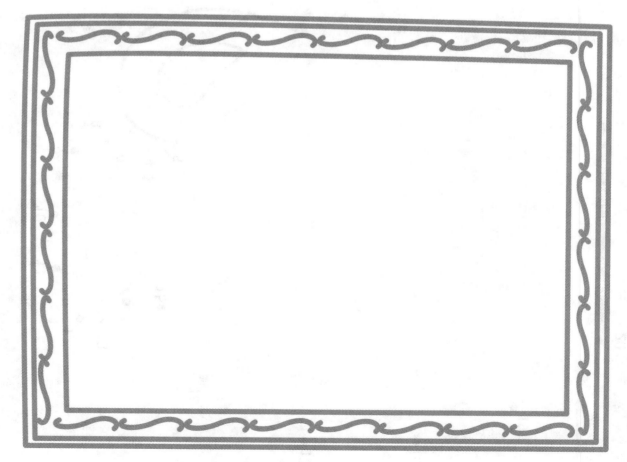

11

Abraham and Sarah laughed when God told them Sarah was going to have a baby, so they named the baby Isaac. Color in the areas with a star to see what "Isaac" means.

Color in the star symbol areas

Sarah and Abraham treated the visitors kindly and gave them food and water. Connect the dots to see how they carried water in Bible times.

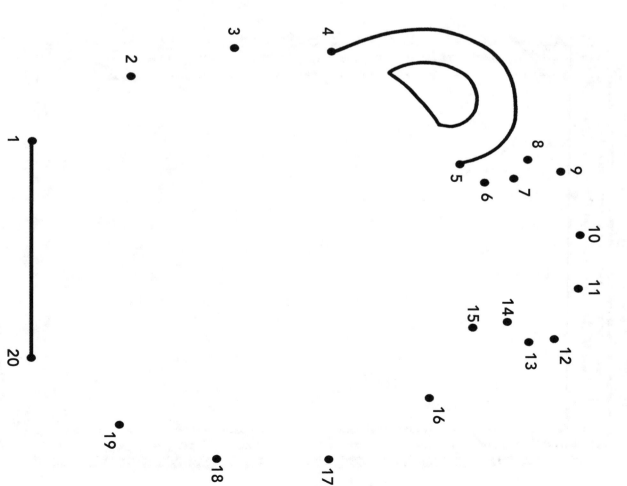

Isaac and Rebekah
Genesis 24:1-67

Abraham decided that it was time for Isaac to get married, so he sent a servant to find a wife for Isaac. When the servant saw that Rebekah was kind and brave, he knew she would be a good wife for Isaac.

The servant prayed for God to help him find Rebekah. Is there something God can help you with? Write or draw it in the frame below.

Help Rebekah find her way to her new home.

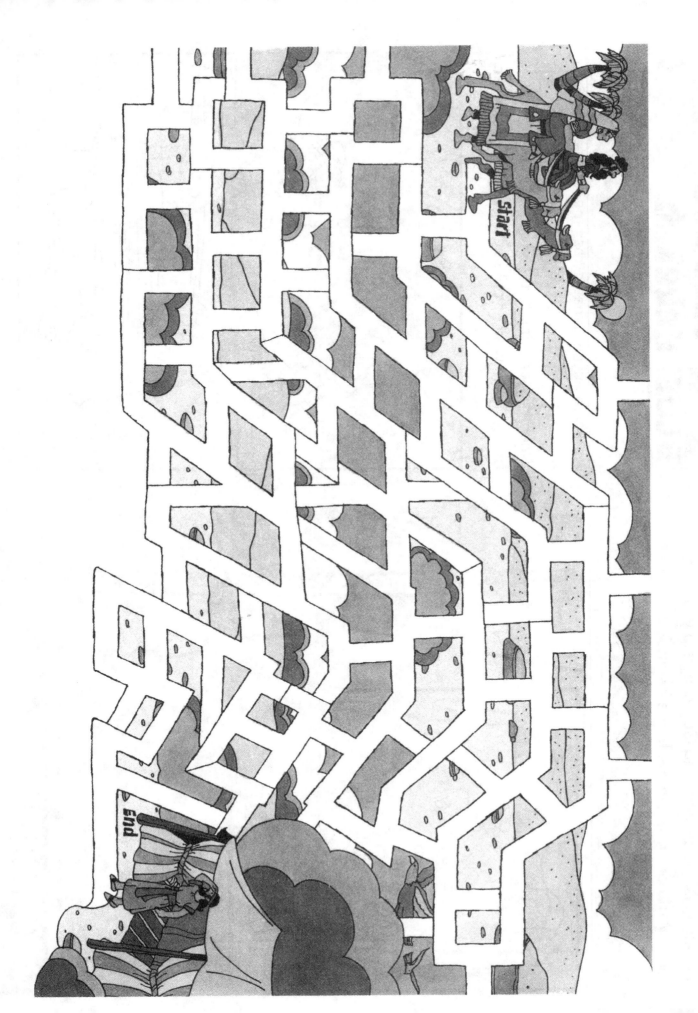

DEEP BLUE Jacob and Esau
Genesis 25:19-28

Isaac and Rebekah had twin boys named Esau and Jacob. Esau was just a few minutes older than Jacob. They looked and acted different from each other.

Do you like to play inside or outside better? Draw a picture of yourself doing your favorite activity.

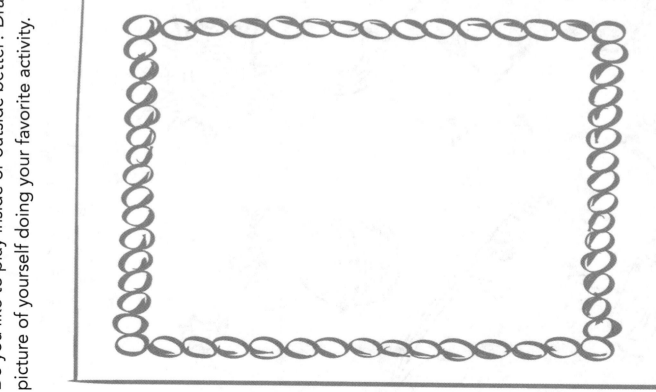

Esau and Jacob were twins but were very different.
Circle the differences between the two pictures.

Esau liked to hunt, fish, and play outdoors.
Jacob liked to be at home and to make food.
Draw a circle around the things that Esau liked
and a square around the things that Jacob liked.

DEEP BLUE
The Birthright
Genesis 25:29-34

Only one son could have the birthright, which meant he would be the leader of the family. Esau was going to be the leader, but Jacob tricked Esau into letting Jacob be the leader.

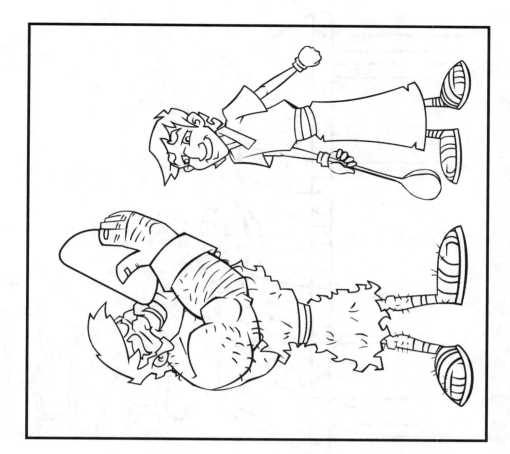

If you were making soup, what would you put in it? Add ingredients to the pot below.

Can you draw in Jacob and Esau?

Help Esau find his way to Jacob's soup.

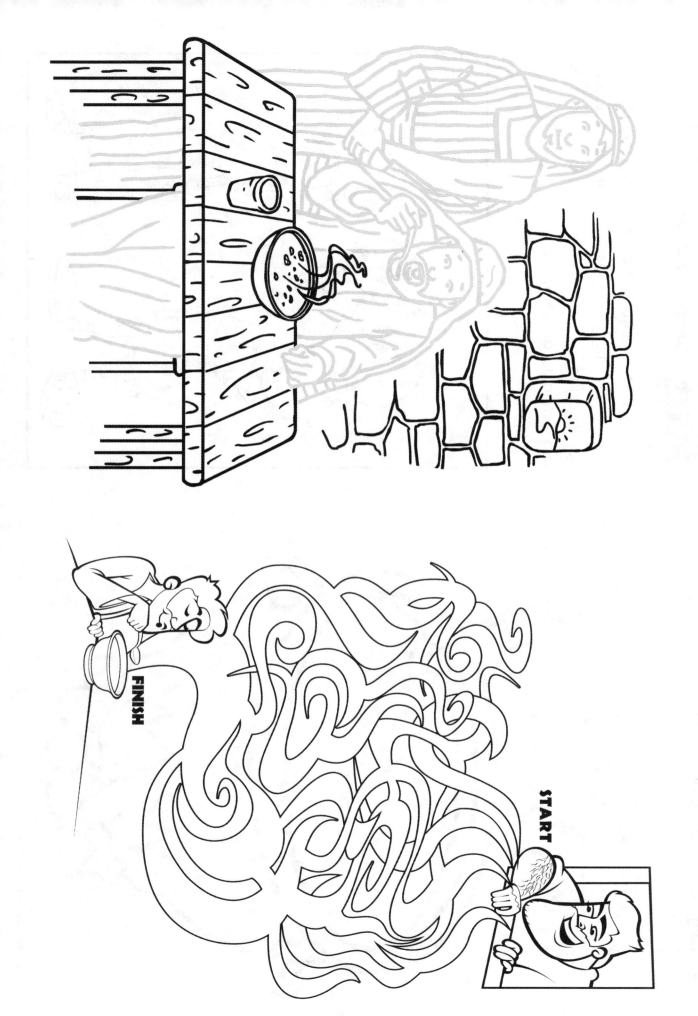

DEEP BLUE

The Blessing
Genesis 27:1-46

Isaac was very old and knew that it was time to give Esau his blessing. Instead, Rebekah helped Jacob get the blessing instead. Esau was very angry!

God blesses all of us! What are some of the blessings in your life? Draw or describe them below.

Copyright © 2017 Abingdon Press

15

Find the twins' twins! Circle the pictures of Jacob and Esau that match exactly.

Color all the spaces marked with a **1** to complete the sentence.

GOD

US

Jacob's Ladder

Genesis 28:10-22

Jacob was scared of Esau, so he ran away. When he went to sleep that night, he had a dream that reminded him that God would always be with him.

In Jacob's dream, angels climbed a ladder to get up and down from heaven. What ways can you imagine angels traveling? Draw or write a story about your answer.

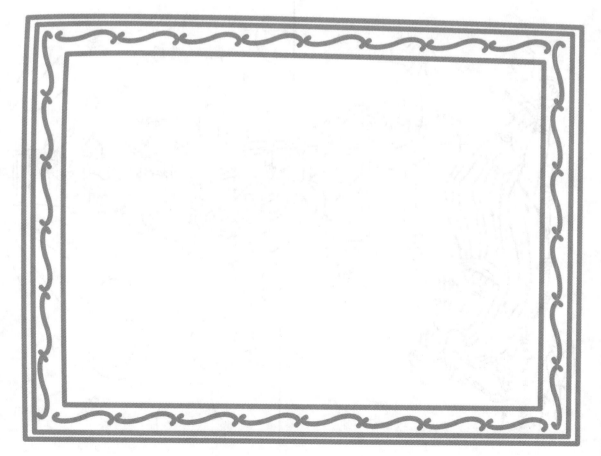

God told Jacob that God would always be with him. God is always with us, too! Color the places where God is with you.

Did you color all of them? God is everywhere!

Count how many there are in the picture.
Angels ___ Stars ___ Rocks ___ Clouds ___

Joseph and His Brothers

Genesis 37:1-36

Jacob had 12 sons. His favorite son was Joseph, but Joseph wasn't kind to his brothers. His brothers got so mad at him that they sold Joseph to be a slave. This made Jacob very sad.

Jacob loved Joseph so much that he gave Joseph a special coat. Imagine what the coat might have looked like. Decorate it below.

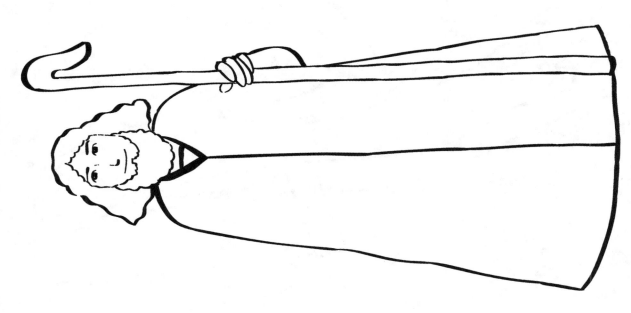

Help Joseph find his coat!

Start

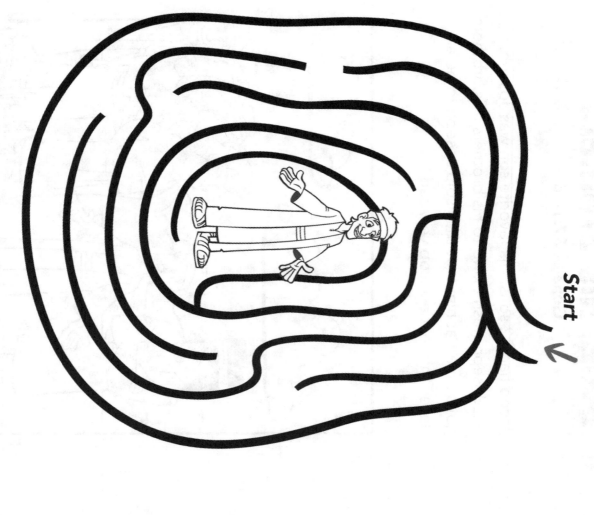

Connect the dots to see Joseph's special coat.

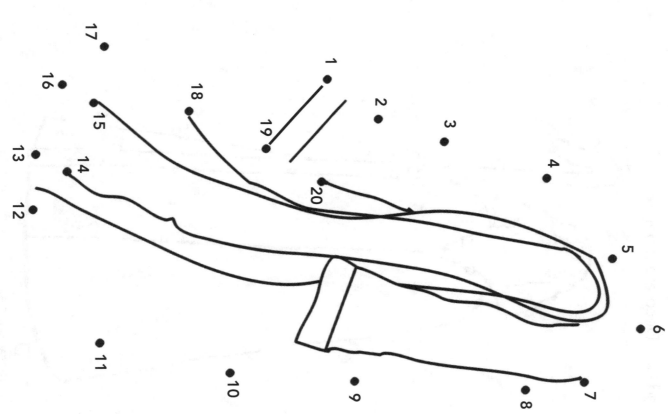

Joseph in Egypt
Genesis 39:1–40:23

In Egypt, Joseph worked for a man named Potiphar. Potiphar's wife told her husband that Joseph did not behave, so Joseph was thrown in jail. In jail, he helped people understand their dreams.

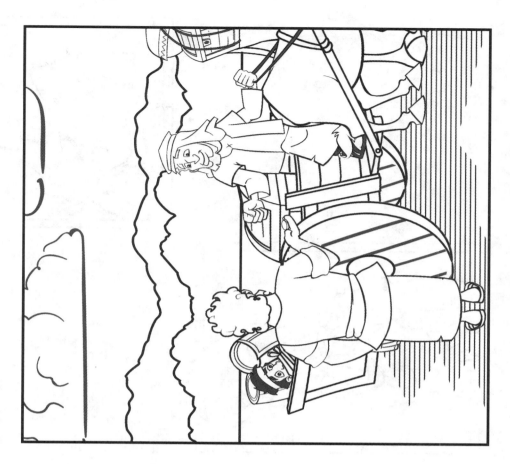

Joseph helped people understand their dreams. He thought that dreams were sometimes messages from God. What do you dream about? Draw a picture of one of your dreams in the dream bubble below.

When he lived in Egypt, Joseph dressed like an Egyptian. Find 6 differences between the two pictures.

Find the words about Joseph in the puzzle below.

L Y R W T M D
B R O T H E R
U E G Y P T E
O C O A T K A
J O S E P H M
W U J A I L S
K E Y T F A D

EGYPT   DREAMS
JOSEPH   COAT
JAIL   BROTHER

Joseph Saves the Day

Genesis 41:1-57

While Joseph was in prison, the Pharoah had two dreams that scared him. Joseph helped him understand the dreams. Joseph knew there would be a time when the people needed food, so Pharoah gave him the job of saving and storing food.

Draw food in the storage areas for Joseph to give away later.

Pharaoh was having lots of dreams.
Connect the dots to see what was in one dream.

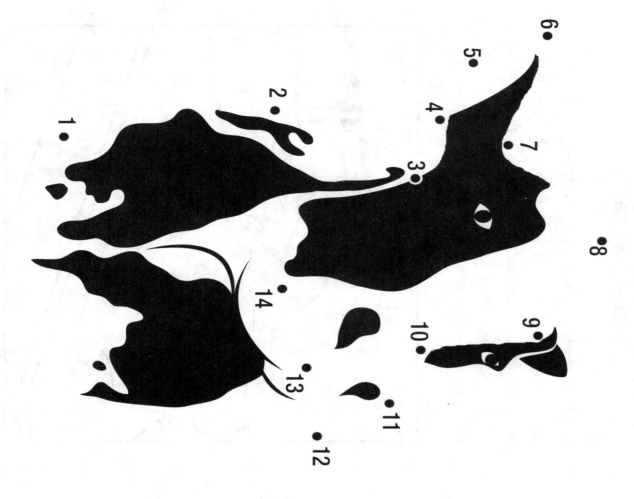

Joseph knew the people of Egypt would run out
of something soon if they didn't do something to
prepare. Cross out the letters in **T-R-E-A-T** to see
what it was.

T	F	R	A	T
E	R	A	O	A
R	O	T	R	E
A	E	R	T	D

Joseph and His Brothers Reunited

Genesis 42:1–46:34

During the famine, Joseph's family in Canaan ran out of food. His brothers went to Egypt to buy more food. They didn't realize they were buying food from Joseph! Joseph finally told his family he was their brother. They celebrated and moved to Egypt to be near Joseph.

Joseph forgave his brothers. Draw a final scene for this story, showing how the boys can forgive each other.

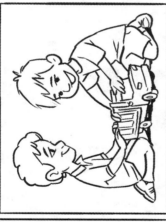

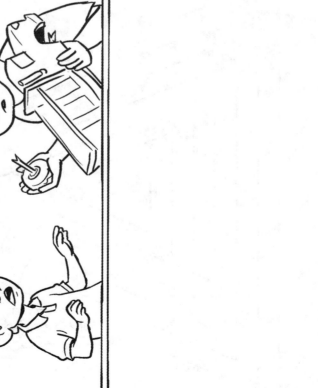

Joseph hid a cup in a sack of grain to make his brothers have to come back to him. Can you find it in the sack below?

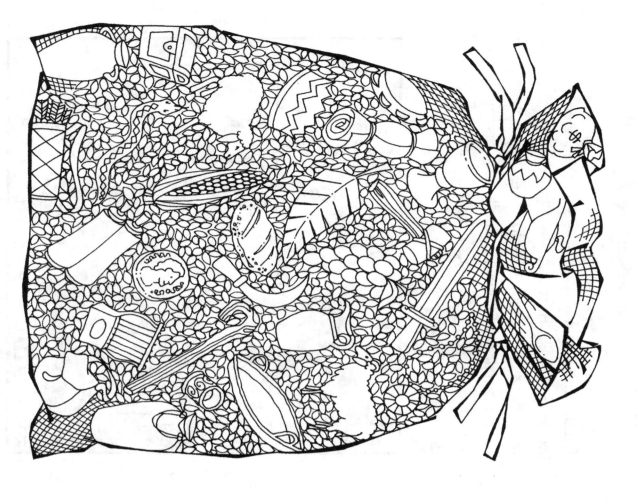

Help Joseph's brothers get back to him.

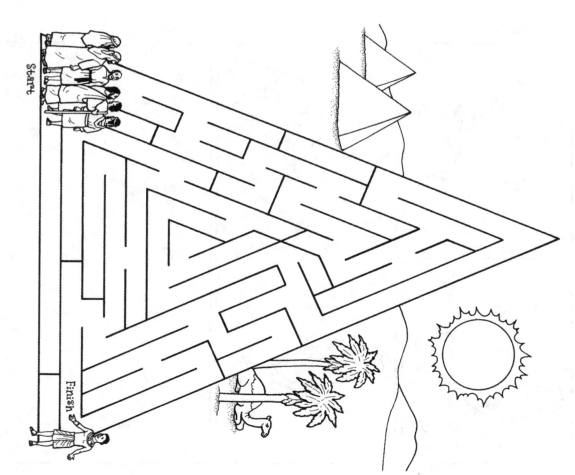

Start

Finish

The Baby in the Basket

Exodus 1:8-14; 2:1-10

After Joseph's family had lived in Egypt for many years, they became slaves again. The king of Egypt, Pharaoh, didn't want the slaves to have babies, but Moses' mother and sister came up with a plan to save baby Moses.

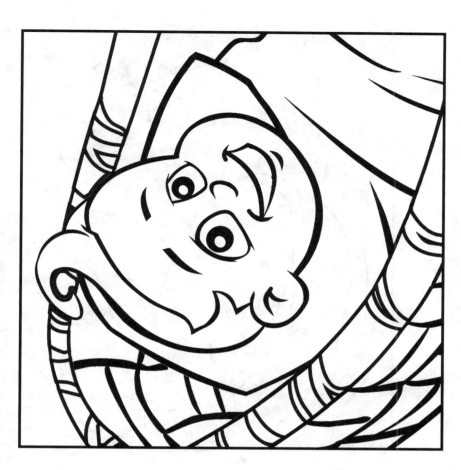

Miriam was Moses' big sister. She helped protect Moses. How can you help protect someone in your life – a brother or sister, a friend, or a pet? Draw the scene in the box below.

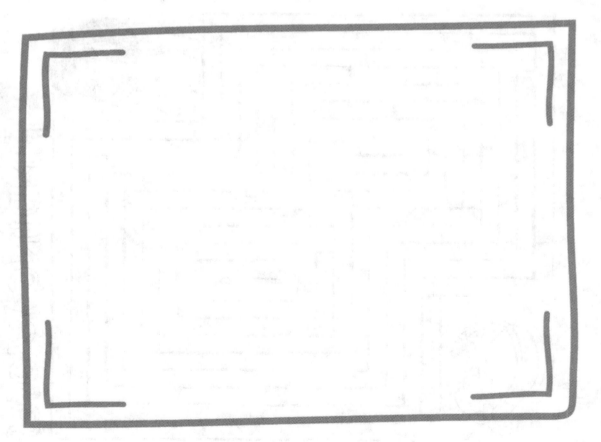

Connect the dots to see Moses in the basket.

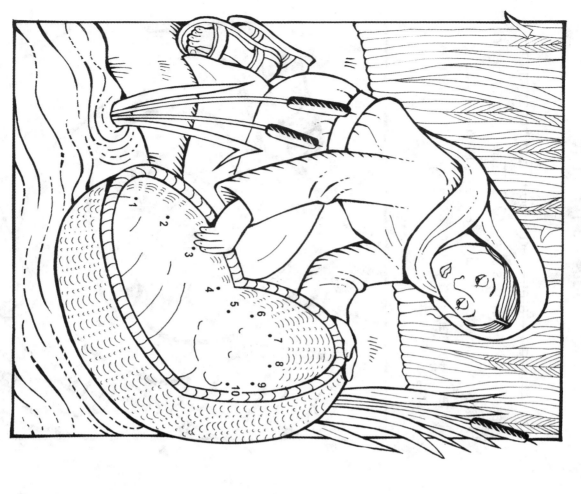

Help Pharaoh's daughter find her way to the baby in the basket.

FINDING MOSES

The Burning Bush

Exodus 2:11–3:22

Moses didn't like how Pharaoh was treating the Hebrew people, making them work as slaves. God had a plan for Moses to help set them free.

God had a big job for Moses. Maybe God has a job for you, too! Draw a picture of something God asks you to do. It can be big or small – what's important is that we listen to God!

Moses was a shepherd.
Help him find his sheep.
Can you also find a
shepherd's hook, a flute,
a pair of sandals, a leather
bucket, a coin, a clay jar,
a bag, and a sling with five
stones?

Complete the picture to show the special way that
God called Moses.

DEEP BLUE

Moses and Pharaoh
Exodus 5:1–13:9

God sent Moses and his brother, Aaron, to tell Pharaoh to let the Israelites go free. Pharaoh refused until God made terrible things happen to the people of Egypt. Then Pharaoh said, "Go!"

Pharaoh was very scared after the terrible things happened. What makes you feel scared? Draw or describe it in the box below. Show it to God and remember that God is always with you, even when you are scared.

God covered Egypt with lots and lots of frogs and bugs. How many frogs and bugs can you find in the picture? Frogs: ____ Bugs: ____

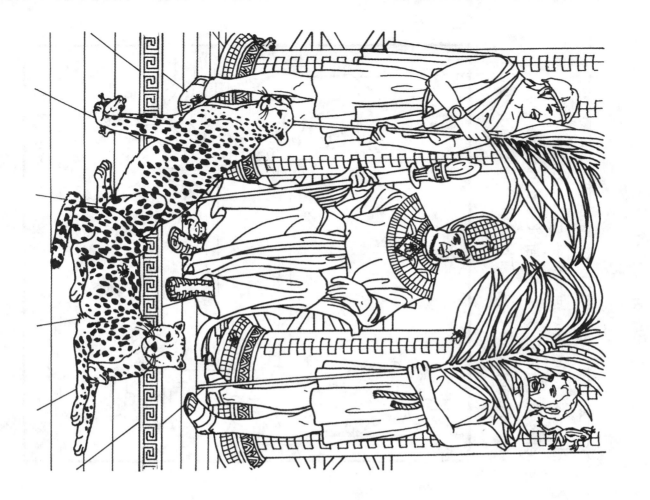

Connect the dots to draw the Pharaoh's throne.

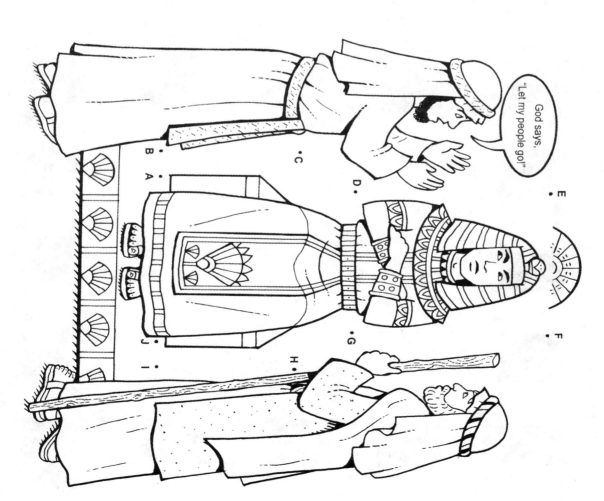

God says, "Let my people go!"

DEEP BLUE
Crossing the Sea
Exodus 13:17–14:31

Pharaoh tried to capture the Israelites again, but God saved them by helping Moses clear a path through the sea.

God kept the Israelites safe from Pharoah's army. Draw something that helps you feel safe.

The Israelites walked right through the Reed Sea.
How many fish can you count in the picture below?

Number these pictures from Moses' life in order.

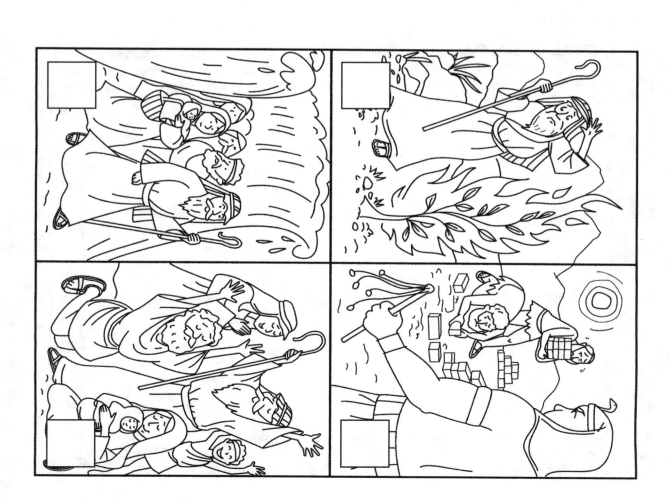

Songs of Joy

Exodus 15:1-21

When the Israelites reached freedom, they were so happy that they worshiped God. Miriam became their song leader.

Miriam led the Israelites in singing because she was so happy. What do you do when you are happy?

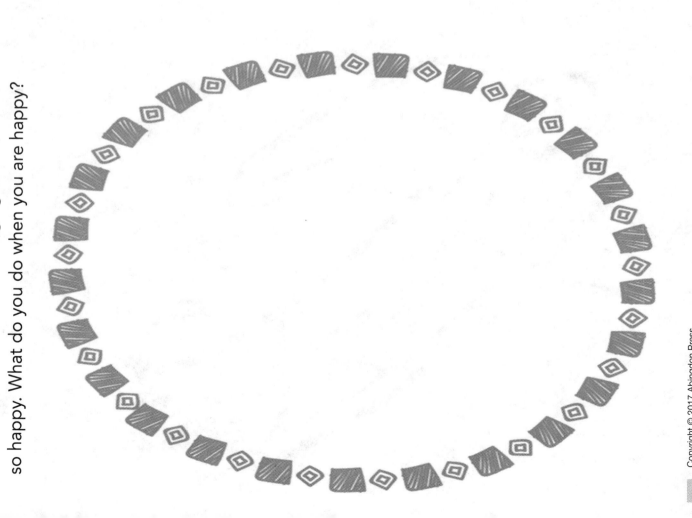

Circle the times when people usually sing.

Finish the picture to see what instrument Miriam played.

The people wondered how they would live in the desert, away from their homes – but God took care of them!

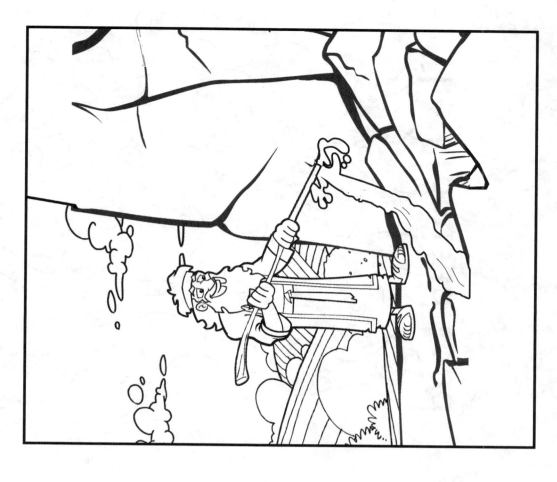

Moses prayed to God, and God gave the Israelites food and water in the desert. Who gives you food and drinks? Draw them in the box below.

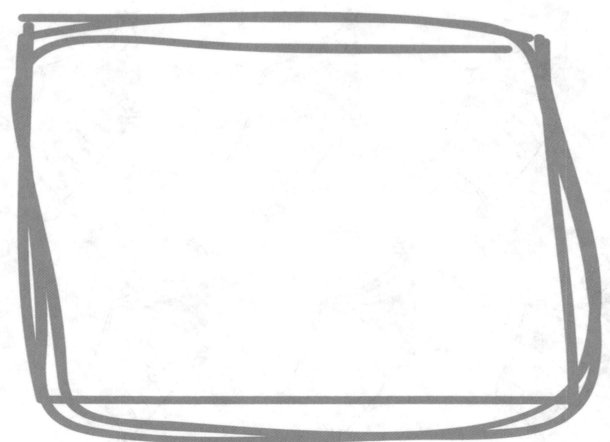

26

Start with the letters at the bottom. Follow each line as far as it goes. If it leads you to a letter, write that letter on the blank below. Fill in all the blanks to see the name of the promised land

BEAYCJNRLNNAGMTAUA

The Promised Land

The Israelites lived in tents in the desert. Can you find the tent that is different from the others?

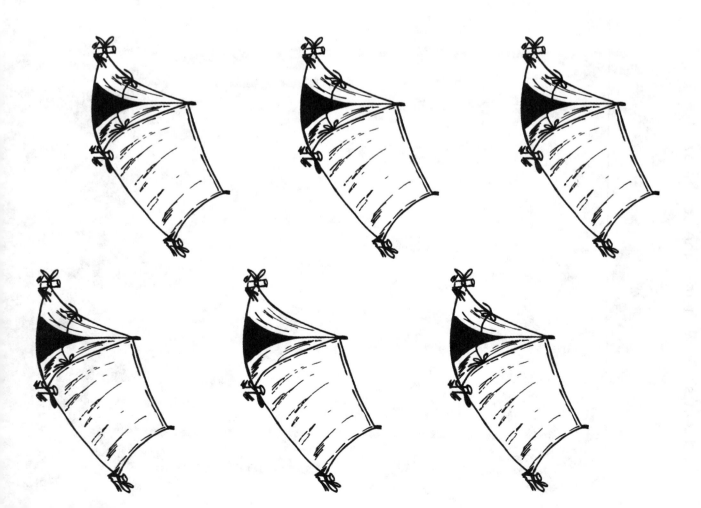

Ten Commandments

Exodus 19:1–20:21

While the Israelites were in the wilderness, God gave them special rules to follow. We call them the Ten Commandments.

The 10 Commandments are God's special rules. They help us love God and love other people well. What is a special rule in your life? Does it help you love God, people, or both? Draw or write the rule in the box below.

Which two pictures of Moses are exactly alike?

Connect the dots to see the tablets God wrote Israel's special rules on. How many commandments did God give Moses? Write the numbers on the tablets.

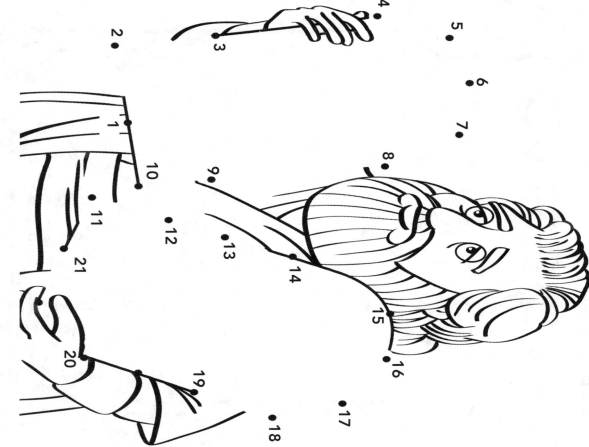

DEEP BLUE

A House for God

Exodus 25:1–31:15, 35:4–40:38

The Israelites worked together to build a special place to worship God. They made a beautiful box, God's special chest, and put the Ten Commandments inside.

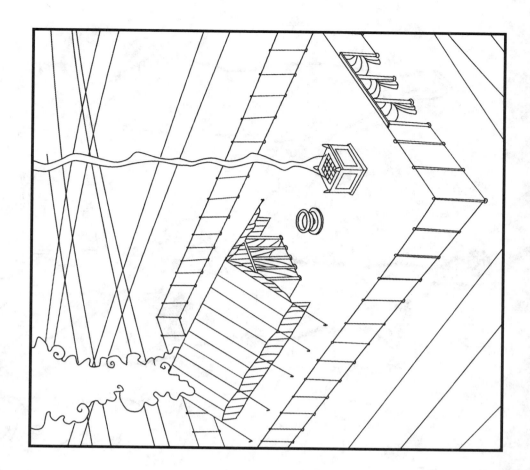

Wandering in the desert, the Israelites built a big tent for God's house. What kind of house would you build for God? Draw it below.

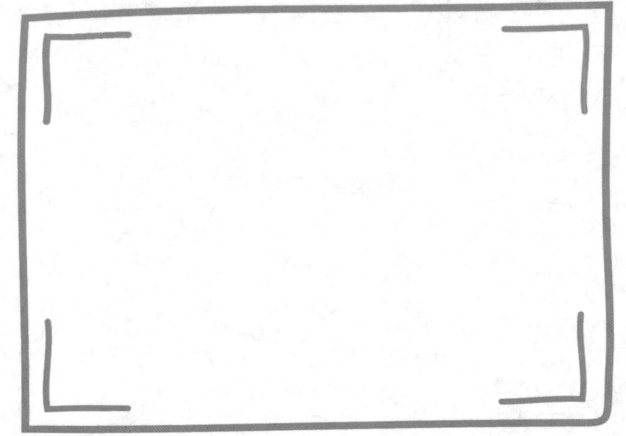

Connect the dots to see what God's special chest might have looked like.

Help the workers bring the materials into the tabernacle.

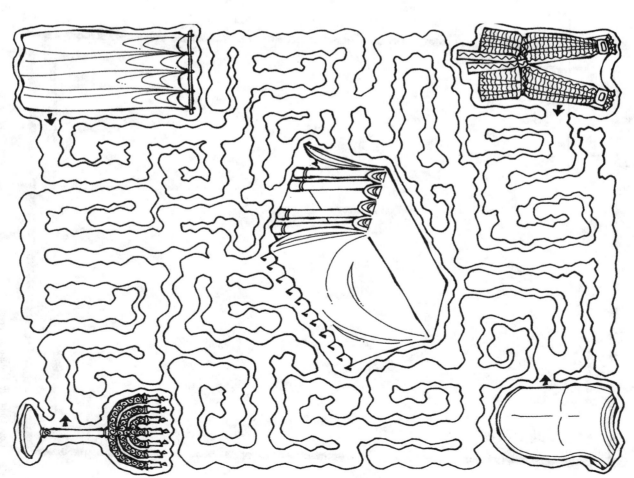

DEEP BLUE

God Chooses Joshua

Joshua 1:1-9

God chose Joshua to be the Israelites' new leader. Moses taught Joshua how to lead the people well.

A leader is someone who helps you know what to do. Who is a leader in your life? Draw him or her below.

Moses is the leader in the top picture. Joshua has become the leader in the bottom picture. What other differences can you find? Circle them.

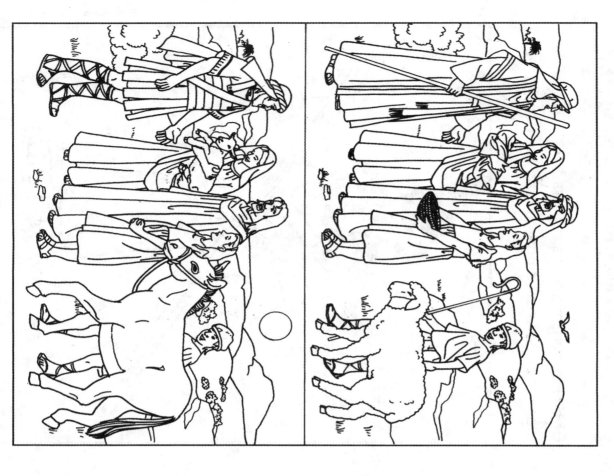

Help Moses show Joshua the way to the promised land.

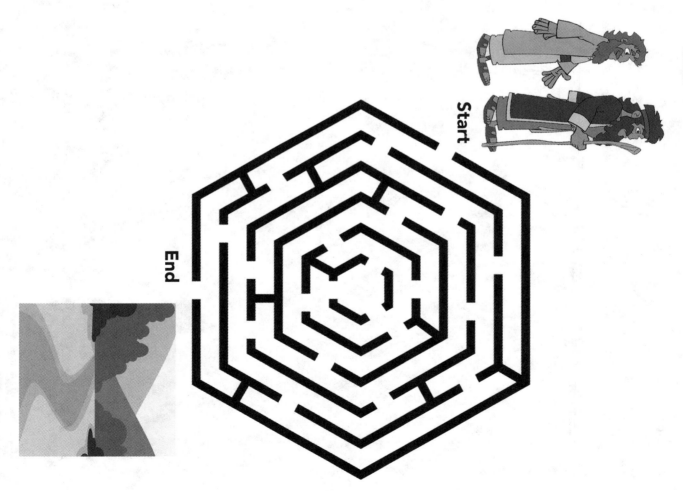

Start

End

Spies in Canaan

Joshua 2:1-24

Joshua sent two men to Jericho to spy on the city. They almost got caught, but a woman named Rahab saved them!

The men hid on Rahab's roof. What's your favorite place to hide? Draw it below.

Connect the dots to see the map of Jericho.

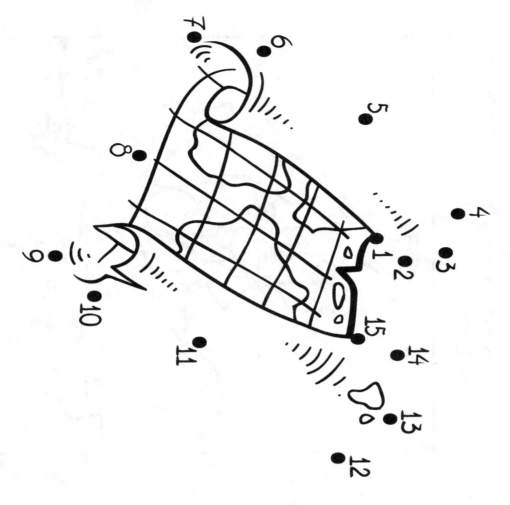

Number these scenes in order of the story.

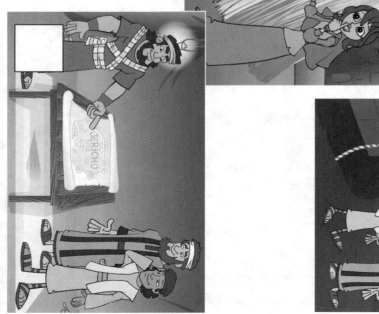

Crossing the Jordan

Joshua 3:1-17; 4:1-24

It was finally time to enter the promised land! The river was flooded, so the people couldn't walk through it – but then God made a path!

The Israelites walked through the Jordan River to get through the promised land. What animals and plants do you think they saw along the way? Add them to the river below.

31

How many men are carrying stones? ____

How many stones are there in all? ____

Draw a circle around the biggest stone.

Draw a square around the smallest stone.

Jericho
Joshua 6:1-27

Even though there was a big wall around Jericho, God broke down the wall and helped the people capture the city. Joshua made sure that Rahab, who had helped the spies, was safe.

The people made a parade and walked around and around the walls of Jericho. Draw a parade in the space below.

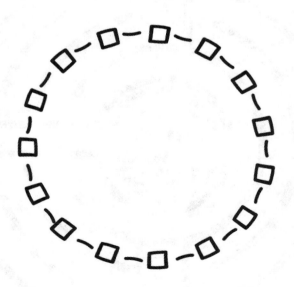

Circle the six objects hidden in the picture of Jericho.

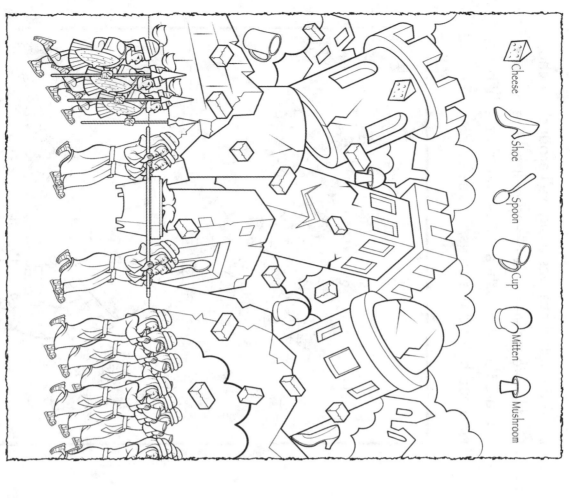

Cheese Shoe Spoon Cup Mitten Mushroom

Follow the path around and into the city.

DEEP BLUE Goodness
Ruth 1–4

Ruth chose kindness. She helped Naomi, and God helped them both.

To help Naomi, Ruth moved to a place she had never been to. When have you gone to a new place? How did you feel? Draw it or write about it below.

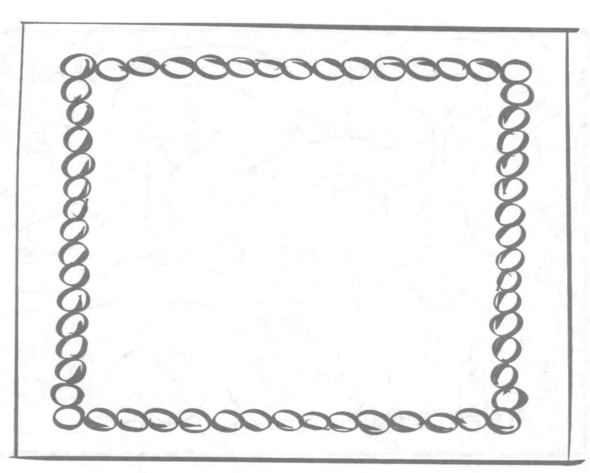

Circle the ways Ruth would have done things.

Naomi and Ruth traveled from Moab to Bethlehem.
Help them find their way.

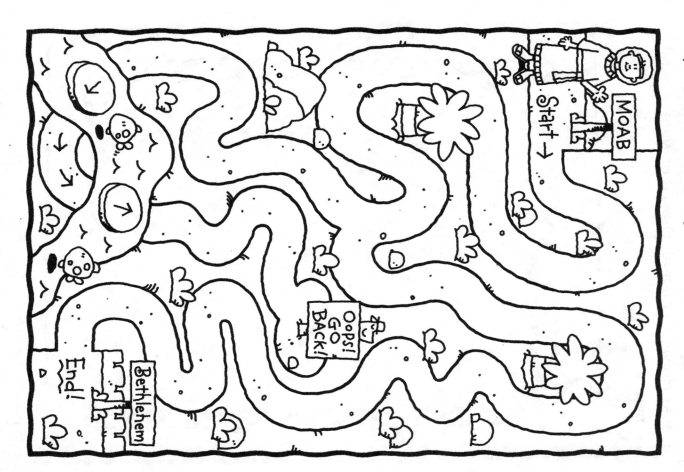

Start →

MOAB

OOPS! GO BACK!

Bethlehem

End!

Hannah Prays
1 Samuel 1:1-28

Hannah was sad that she didn't have any children. She prayed for God to give her a child. God gave her Samuel!

Samuel was the best present Hannah ever received. What's the best present you have been given? Draw it or write about it below.

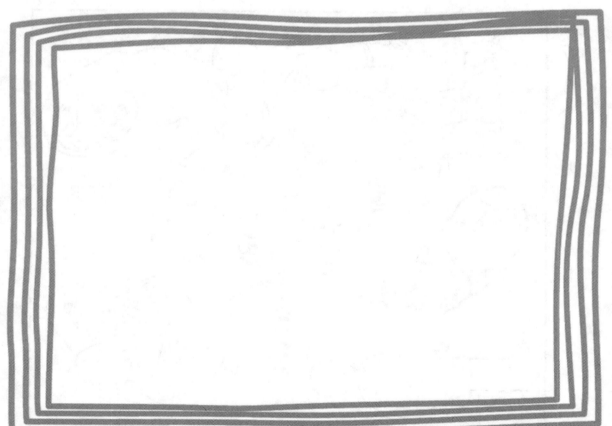

Hannah went to the temple to pray for a baby. Help her find her way through the maze to the temple.

Draw a line from the picture to the word it matches.

BABY

PRAY

MOM

BOY

SAD

God calls Samuel

1 Samuel 3:1-21

Samuel heard somebody calling him. He thought it was Eli, the priest, but it was actually God! God had big plans for Samuel.

God calls us by speaking to our hearts. People use phones to call each other. Draw a phone below. Who would you call?

Hannah and Samuel traveled from their home to the Temple in Shiloh. Show them the way.

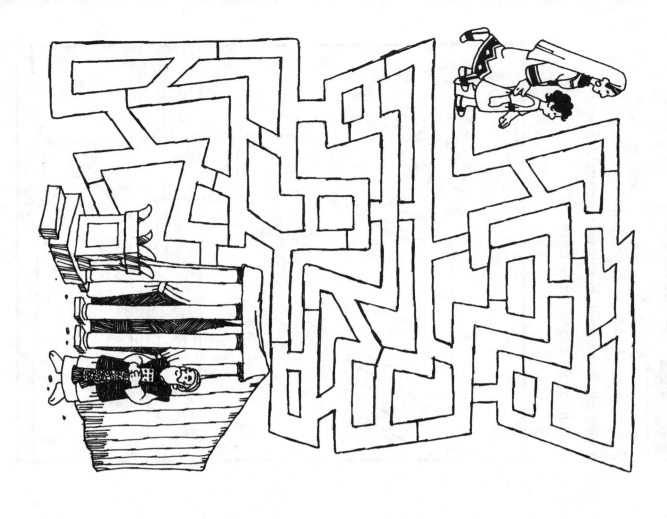

Circle the 5 things that are different in the two pictures of Samuel hearing God's call.

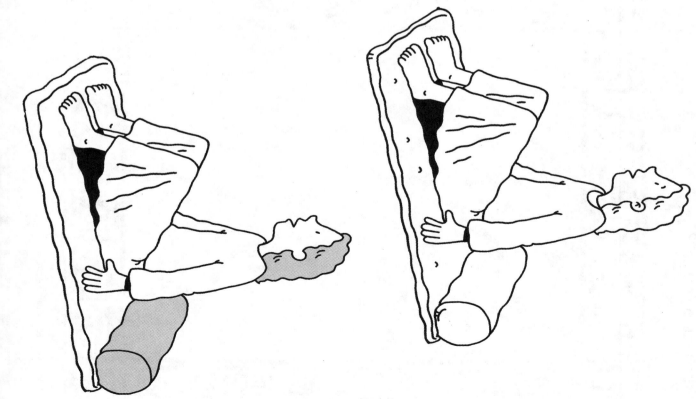

DEEP BLUE

Samuel Anoints Saul

1 Samuel 7:15–8:22; 10:17-24

When Samuel grew up, he became a leader of his people. The people decided they wanted to have a king, so Samuel listened to God's voice and chose Saul to become the king.

Saul became Israel's first king. If you were a king or queen, what would you wear on your head? Add it below.

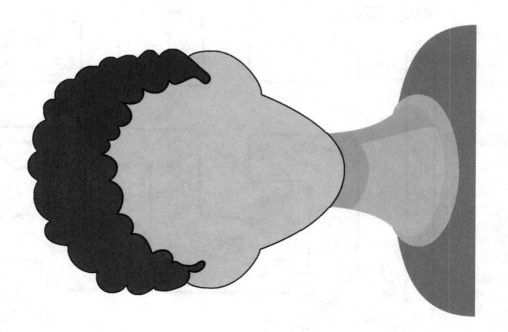

When Saul heard that Samuel was looking for him, he hid. Can you find Saul in the picture below?

Help Samuel find Saul.

Samuel Anoints David

1 Samuel 16:1-23

Saul disobeyed God, so the people needed a new king. God told Samuel to choose David as the one who would become king by pouring oil on his head as a sign of God's blessing. Samuel chose David even though David was the youngest of all his brothers.

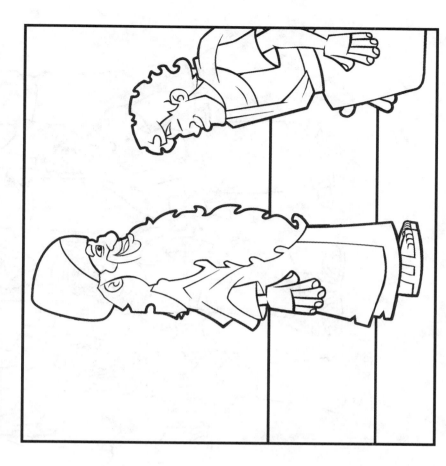

David made God's heart happy. Draw yourself doing something that makes God happy.

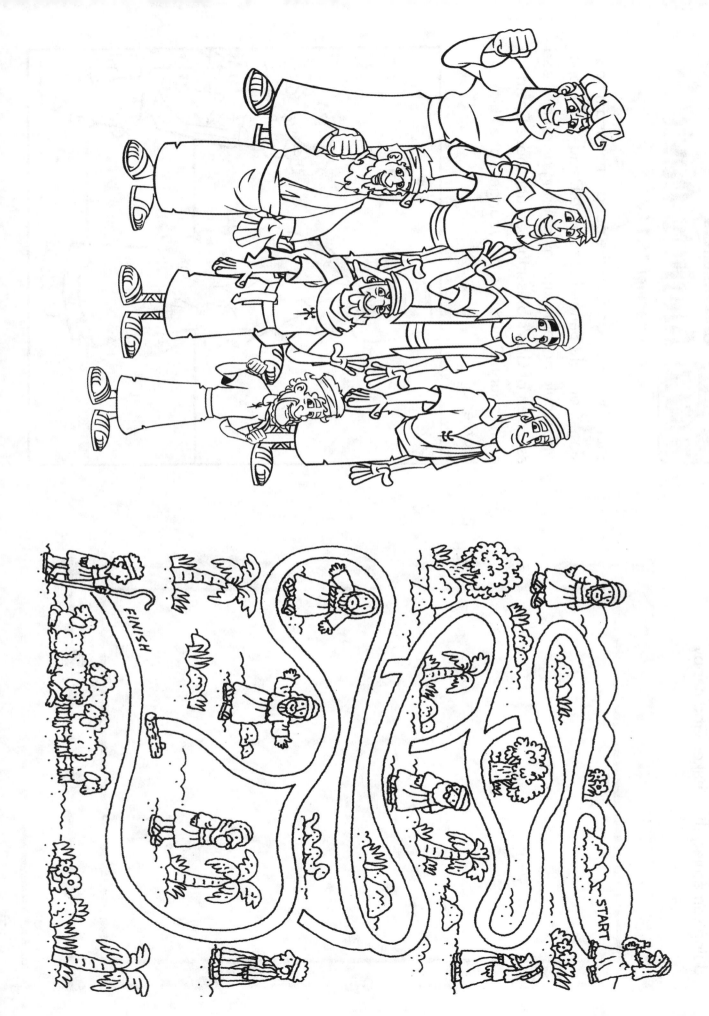

David was the smallest brother. Circle David below.

Help Samuel find his way to David.

START

FINISH

David the Musician

1 Samuel 16:14-23

King Saul had nightmares at night and unhappy thoughts during the day. When David would play music for him, King Saul felt much better.

Trace the music notes and add more of your own.

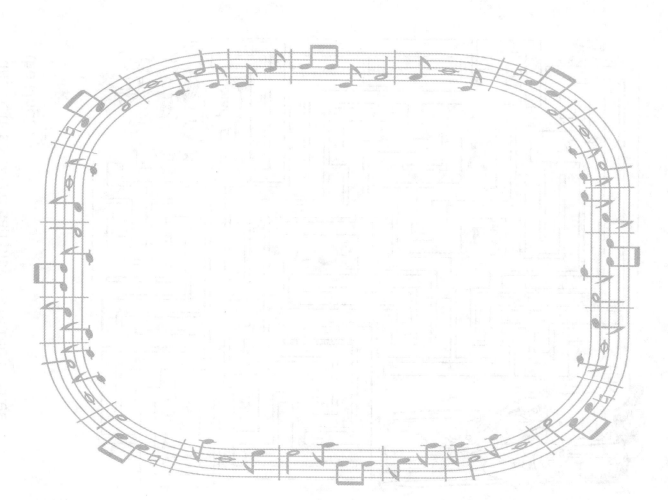

Can you find five musical instruments in the picture? Circle them.

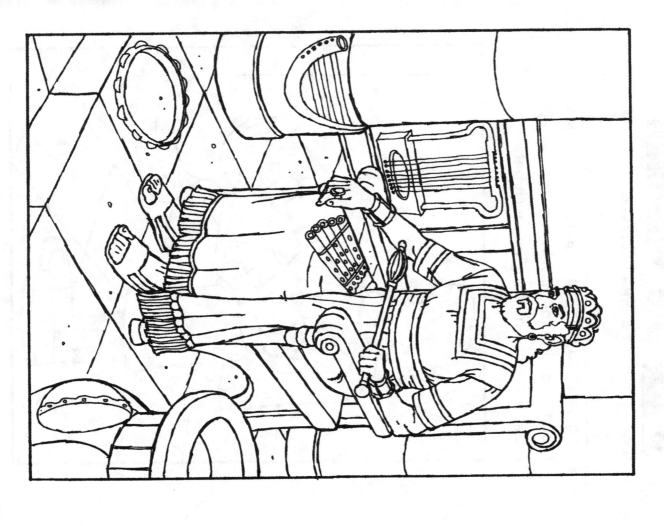

Find the path through the maze from David to King Saul so David can play his music to cheer up the king.

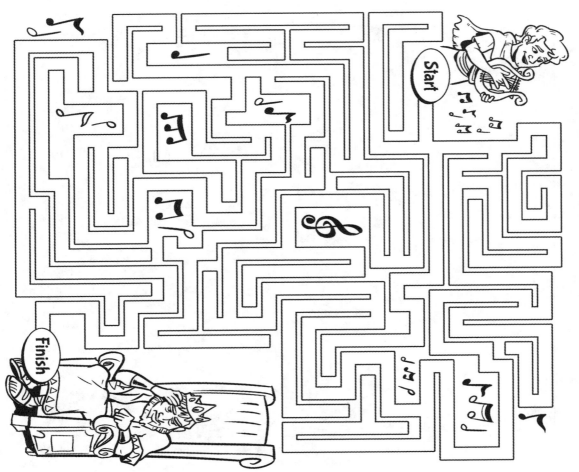

Start

Finish

David and Goliath

1 Samuel 17:1-51a

David was brave enough to fight Goliath, who was very, very big. With God's help, David defeated Goliath even though the bigger and stronger soldiers couldn't!

Goliath was nine feet tall! How tall do you think David was? Draw him next to Goliath.

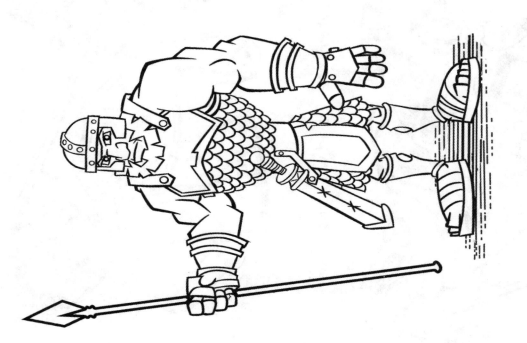

Find two identical giants.

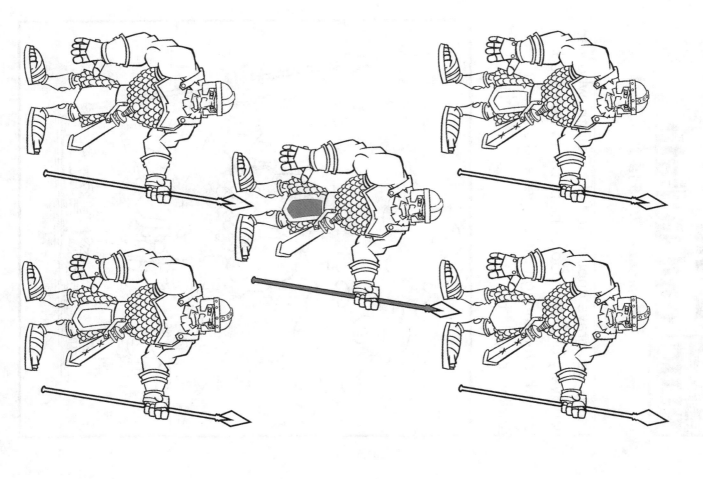

Circle the items that Goliath would have used.

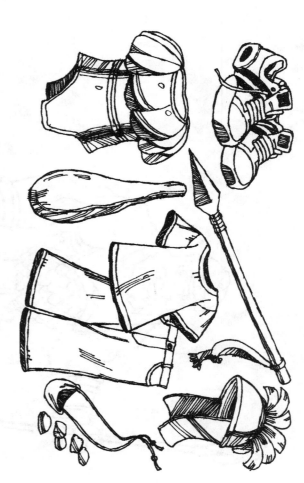

Circle the items that David would have used.

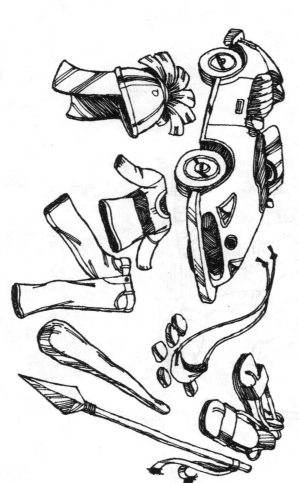

DEEP BLUE

David and Jonathan

1 Samuel 18:1-5; 20:1-42

David and Jonathan were best friends. Jonathan's dad, King Saul, got very mad at David, so Jonathan helped David to safety.

Draw you and one of your best friends.

Jonathan gave David a very special gift.
Solve the puzzle to discover the gift. Start with
A and count the letters. Find the letter that goes
with the number given and write it in the blank.

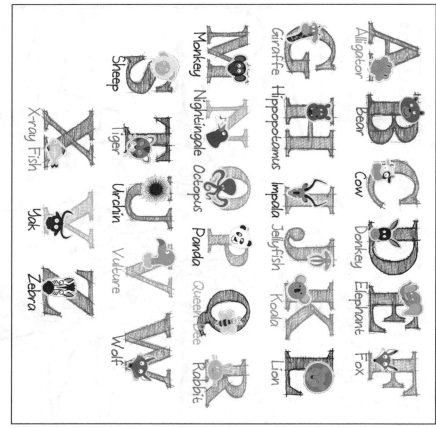

A Alligator B Bear C Cow D Donkey E Elephant F Fox
G Giraffe H Hippopotamus I Impala J Jellyfish K Koala L Lion
M Monkey N Nightingale O Octopus P Panda Q Queen Bee R Rabbit
S Sheep T Tiger U Urchin V Vulture W Wolf
X X-ray Fish Y Yak Z Zebra

| ___ | ___ | ___ | ___ | ___ |
| 6 | 18 | 9 | 5 | 14 |

| ___ | ___ | ___ | ___ | ___ |
| 4 | 19 | 8 | 9 | 16 |

Draw a heart beside the children who are acting
like friends. Put an X beside the children who are
not being friends.

David and Abigail

1 Samuel 25:1-42

David had a fight with a man named Nabal. Nabal's wife, Abigail, helped them stop fighting. Abigail was a peacemaker.

We all get angry sometimes, and that's okay. Draw something that makes you angry.

Abigail brought David and his men lots of food. Circle the items that Abigail might have brought them, then add those items to the donkey's back.

Abigail made peace between David and Nabal. Circle the kids who are acting peacefully.

DEEP BLUE David Dances
2 Samuel 6:1-19

After David became king, he was able to bring the God's special chest into the city of Jerusalem. This made him so happy that he danced at the front of the parade to praise God.

Have you ever seen a parade? Draw one below!

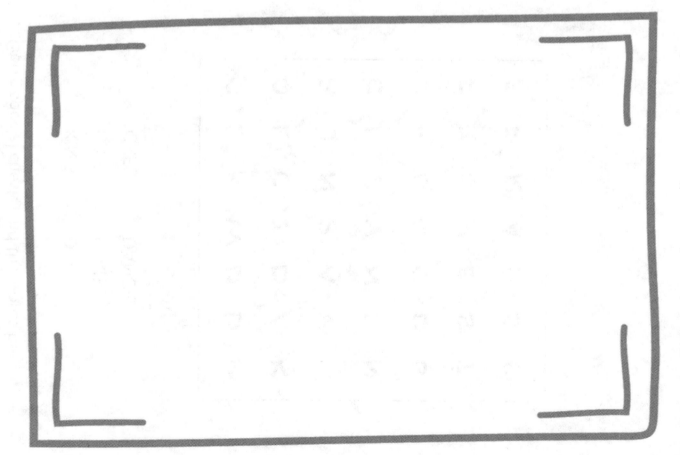

Help David dance his way into the city!

David praised God by dancing into the city in front of God's special chest. Find the words below.

KING   DAVID
CITY   PRAISE
CHEST   DANCE

O	L	K	W	D	D	P
Q	L	C	N	D	A	K
F	U	N	P	A	V	I
C	I	T	Y	N	I	N
Q	F	D	Q	C	D	G
P	N	C	H	E	S	T
F	P	R	A	I	S	E

Kindness
2 Samuel 9:1-13

King David had not forgotten his friend Jonathan. He gave Jonathan's son, Mephibosheth, everything he needed. King David was very kind!

Draw a picture of something kind you can do for a family member this week.

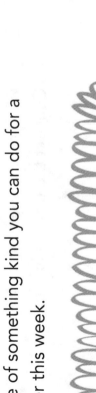

Which kids are showing kindness? Circle them.

What do we share when we are kind?
Connect the dots to find out.

13
14
15
1
2
3
4
5
6
7
8
9
10
11
12

Solomon Becomes King

1 Kings 2:1-4; 3:1-15

When Solomon became king, he asked God for wisdom. God helped Solomon.

Imagine that you became queen or king. What's the first thing you would do? Describe or draw it below.

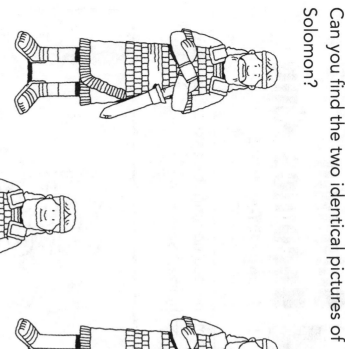

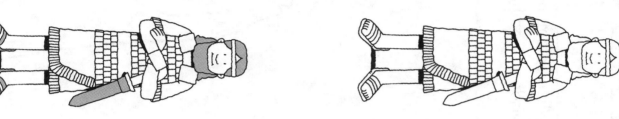

Help Solomon find his way to his new throne.

Solomon Builds the Temple

1 Kings 6:1-38

Solomon and the Israelites built a special place to worship God, called the Temple.

The Temple was like a very big church. What does your church look like? Draw or describe it below.

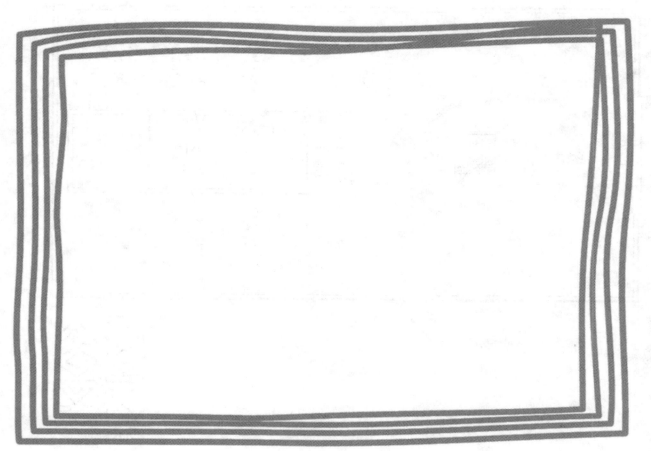

Can you find these five shapes in the Temple?
Color each shape a different color.

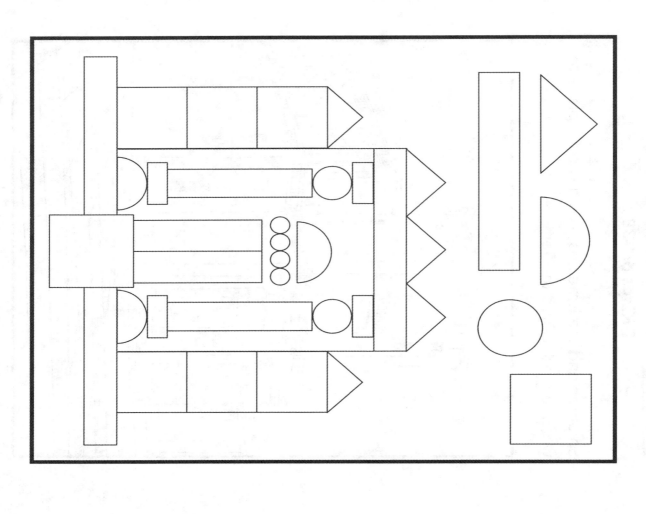

The ark of the covenant goes behind the veil in the
Holy of Holies. Can you draw it where it belongs?

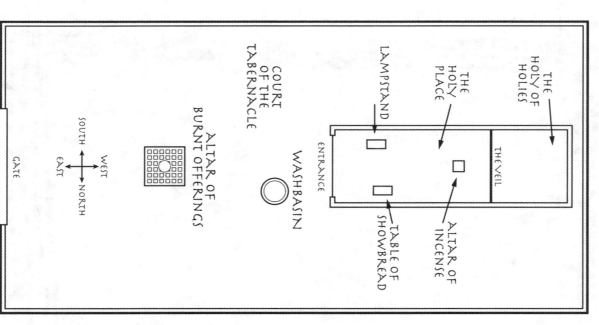

COURT
OF THE
TABERNACLE

LAMPSTAND

THE
HOLY
PLACE

THE
HOLY OF
HOLIES

ENTRANCE

WASHBASIN

THE VEIL

TABLE OF
SHOWBREAD

ALTAR OF
INCENSE

ALTAR OF
BURNT OFFERINGS

SOUTH

WEST   EAST

NORTH

GATE

GOD'S
HOUSE

DEEP BLUE

Solomon Dedicates the Temple

1 Kings 6:1-68

Solomon and the people had the first worship service in the Temple they had built.

We can pray anywhere! Where is somewhere you like to pray? Draw or describe it below.

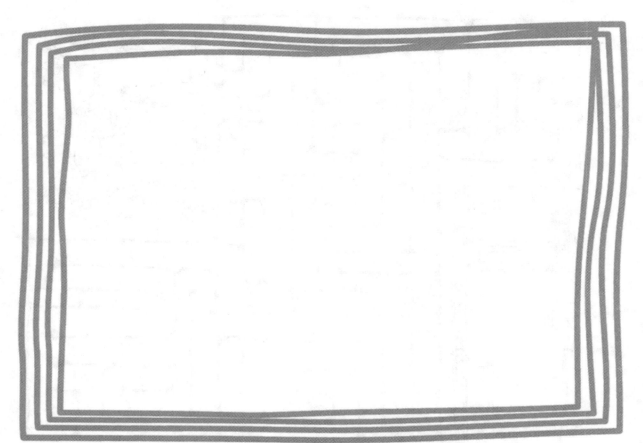

Connect the dots to see how the Temple was built.

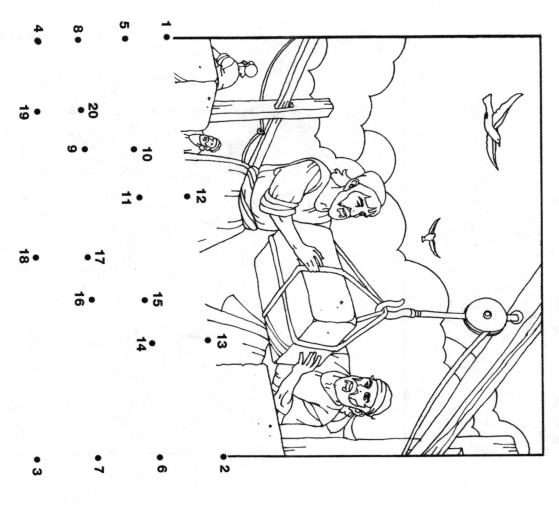

Help the family find their way to the Temple.

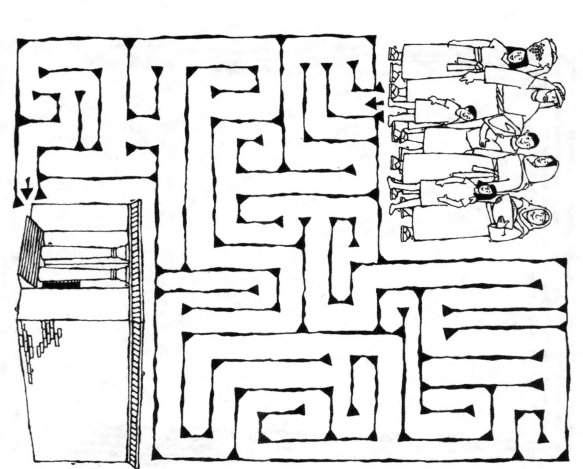

Elijah and the Ravens

1 Kings 16:29-30; 17:1-7

Elijah was a prophet who spoke up when things were unfair. He helped people know what God wanted them to do. The king didn't like what Elijah said. God used birds carrying food to take care of Elijah, even when the king was mad at him.

Elijah didn't have food to eat! Draw some food for him below.

God supplied Elijah's needs to eat and drink. Circle the items God gave to Elijah, then add them to the picture.

How many ravens can you find in the picture?

Answer: _____

Elijah and the Prophets

1 Kings 18:20-39

When Elijah prayed for God to make a fire, God did it and showed everybody that God is the one true God.

In order to show God's power, God made a fire on Elijah's altar. Add the fire below.

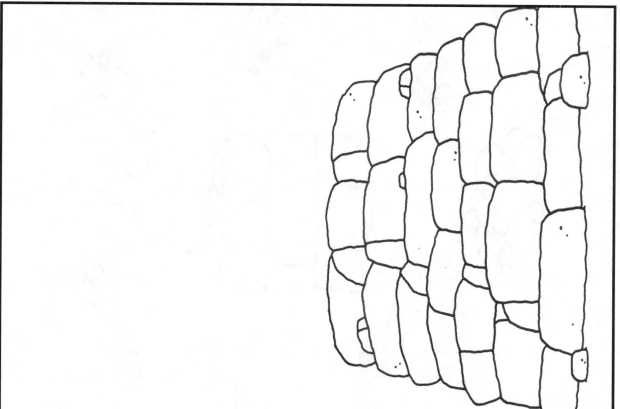

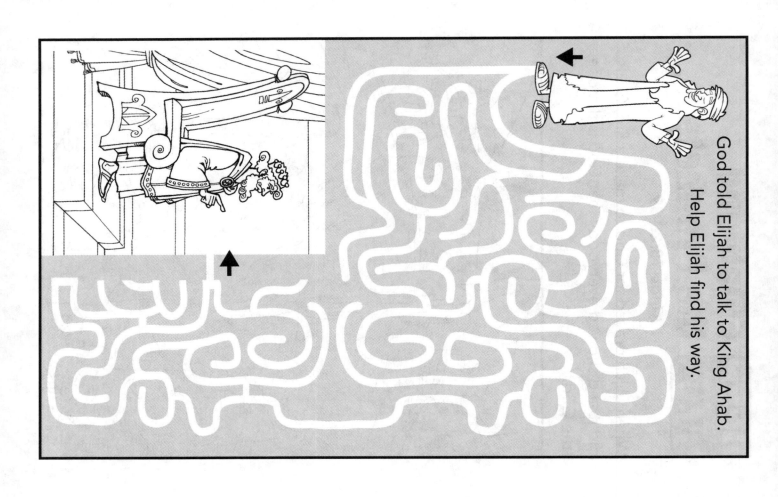

God told Elijah to talk to King Ahab.
Help Elijah find his way.

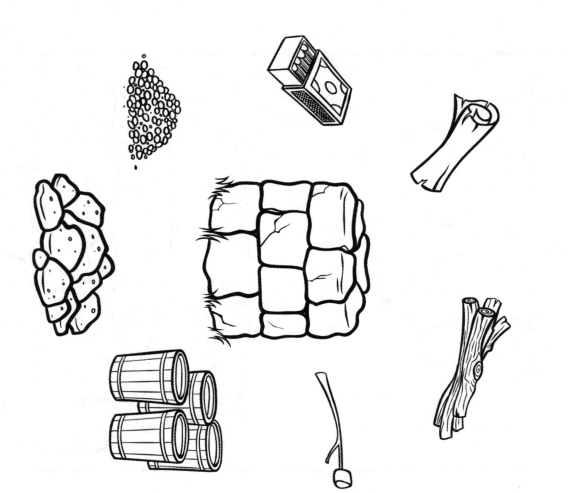

What did Elijah need to start the fire on his altar?
Circle the items he may have used.

Faithfulness
2 Kings 22:1–23:23

The Israelites had forgotten God's rules. King Josiah helped the people worship God again.

King Josiah was faithful and loved God. Draw a picture that shows how much you love God.

Josiah helped his people pray to God. Trace the praying hands.

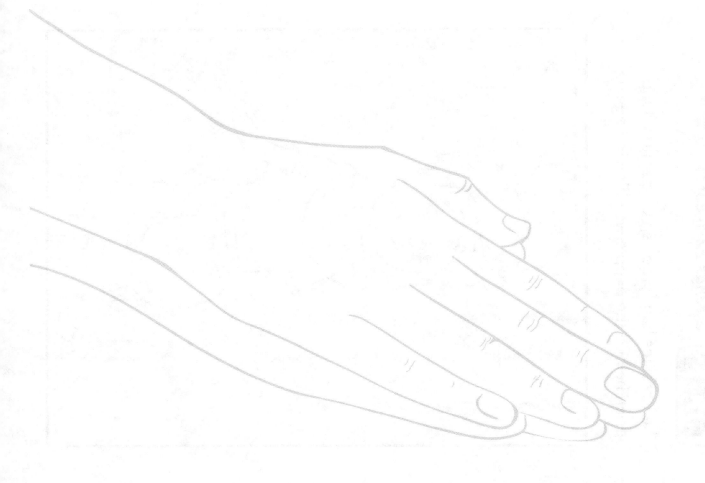

King Josiah found a scroll that reminded the people how God wanted them to live. Connect the dots to add the scroll to the picture.

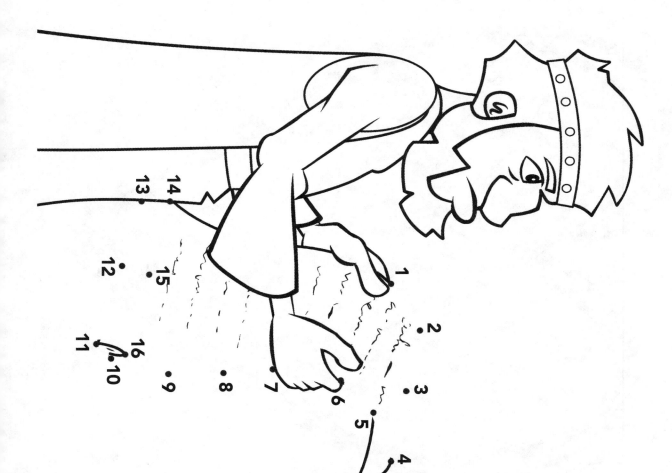

Elisha and the Widow's Jars

2 Kings 4:1-7

Elisha was a prophet who spoke up when things were unfair and helped people know what God wanted them to do. Elisha helped a small family get the food they needed.

The widow and her children were happy when they had food to eat! What is your favorite food? Draw it below.

Elisha told the widow to borrow as many jars as she could, then to fill them with oil. Count the number of jars below. Write the number on the blank at the bottom of the page.

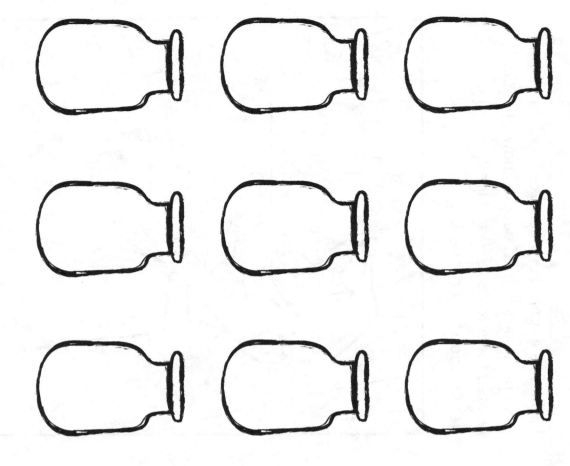

Circle the objects that use oil. Then color the picture.

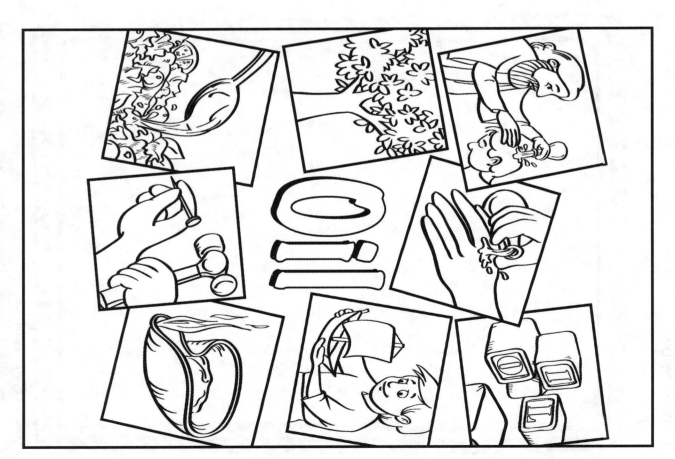

Elisha and the Servant Girl

2 Kings 5:1-19

Elisha, a prophet, healed a sick man. The servant girl helped!

Even though the servant was young, she helped in a big way. What's a way you can help when someone is sick? Draw it below.

51

Help Naaman find his way on his journey to see Elisha.

Naaman went to see Elisha at his house for healing. Which numbers are missing in the houses below?

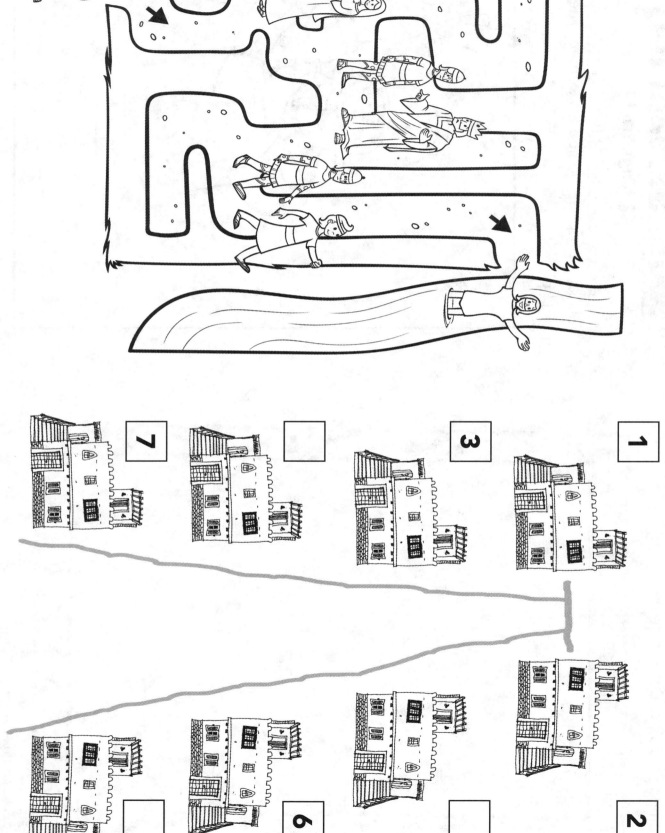

Courageous Queen

Esther 1–8

Queen Esther was smart and brave. God helped her save her people!

Esther had to be brave in a scary time.
Draw something that scares you.
Then draw yourself being brave!

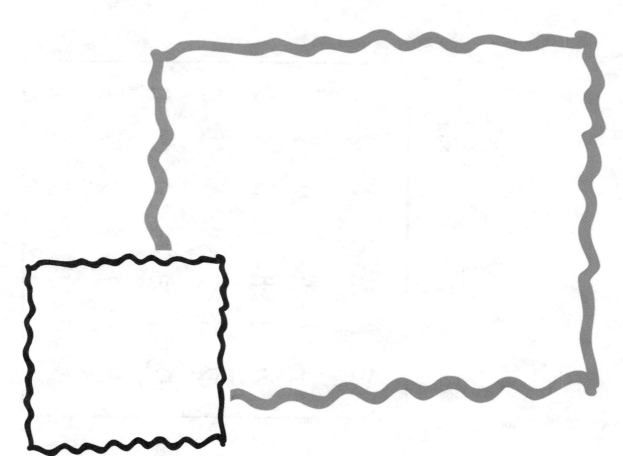

Connect the dots to see Queen Esther's crown.

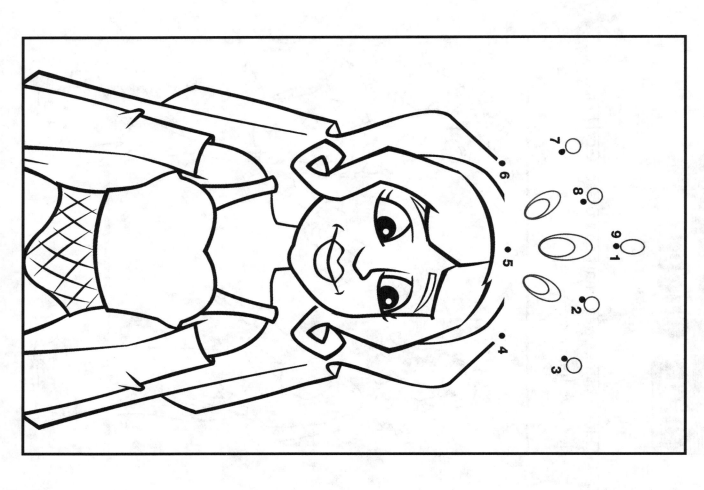

Esther invited the king and Haman to have dinner with her. Find the words hidden in the puzzle below.

```
Z  P  O  K  I  N  G
X  A  C  A  I  Y  M
U  Q  U  E  E  N  G
D  I  N  N  E  R  Q
C  E  S  T  H  E  R
H  A  M  A  N  T  R
U  C  R  O  W  N  E
```

KING   DINNER
QUEEN   ESTHER
CROWN   HAMAN

DEEP BLUE Gentleness
Psalm 23:1-6

God is like a shepherd. We are like God's sheep.
God takes care of us.

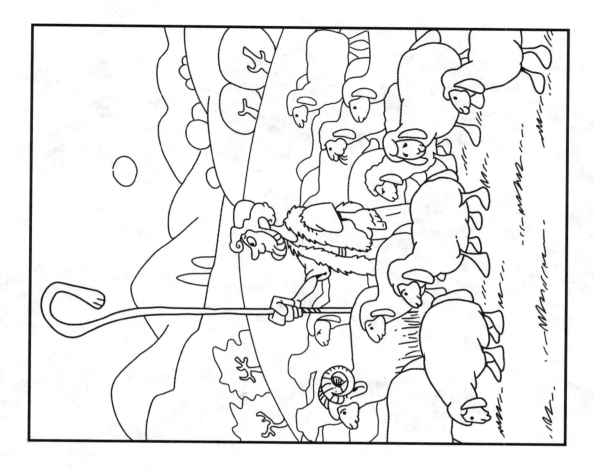

Some animals are fierce, like a tiger. Some animals are gentle, like sheep. Draw a gentle animal below.

53

Circle the pictures of people being gentle and draw an X over the pictures of people being rough.

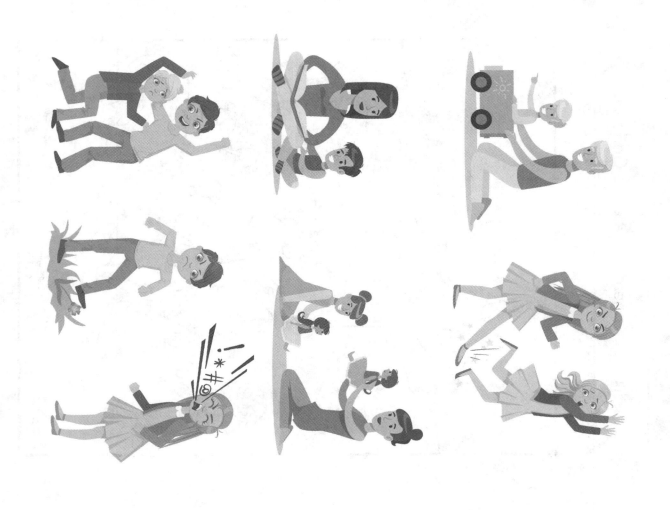

Circle the sheep who needs help. Help the shepherd find the hurt sheep by connecting them with a line.

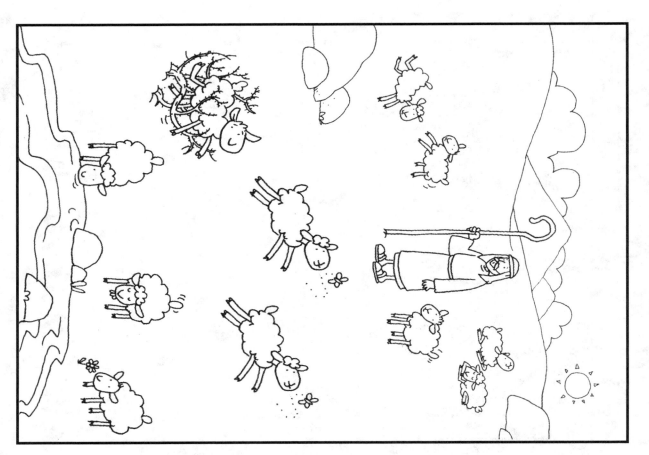

DEEP BLUE

Joy
Psalm 100:1-5

We worship the Lord with joy!

There is so much joy in God's world!
Draw whatever makes you happy!

Which suns look happy? Which suns look unhappy?
Circle the suns that are joyful.

Color the instruments from Bible times in one color; instruments from today in another color; and instruments that were used in Bible times that we still use today in a third color.

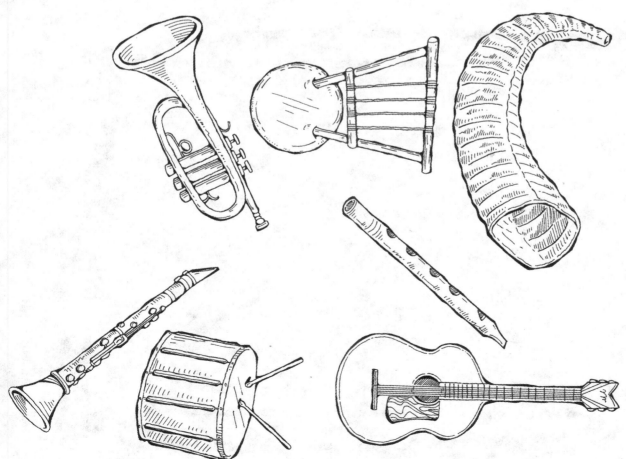

Solomon's Wisdom Proverbs

Proverbs 6:6-8; 10:1; 17:17

Solomon helped his people make wise choices.

Who's the wisest person you know? Draw him or her below.

Can you find 5 differences between the two pictures?

Put a checkmark beside each child who is making a wise decision.

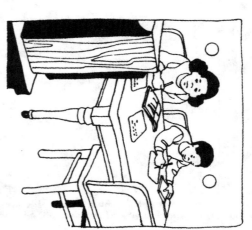

DEEP BLUE
The Peaceable Kingdom
Isaiah 11:6-9

Someday all of God's creation will live in peace!

Trace the drawing below. This is the peace sign. Add more peace signs. Can you cover the whole page in peace signs like God's peace will cover the whole world?

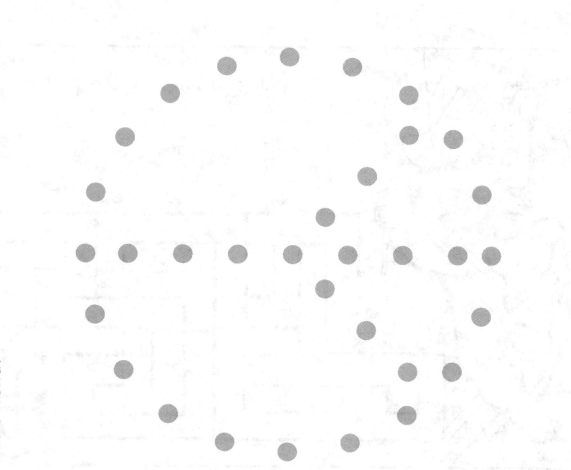

You can be a peacemaker!
Circle the kids who are behaving kindly.

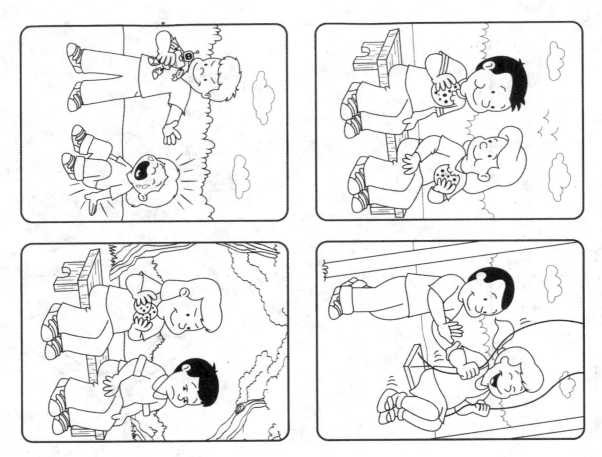

Help the lamb find its way to the lion.

DEEP BLUE
A Baby Is Coming
Jeremiah 23:5-8

Jeremiah told the people that someday a baby would be born who would become their best king ever.

Jeremiah wrote about a baby that would be born and become a king. Add a crown to the baby below.

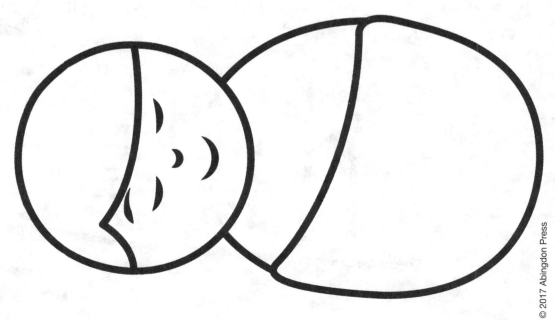

The baby who would be born would be very special! Find the baby who looks different from the other ones.

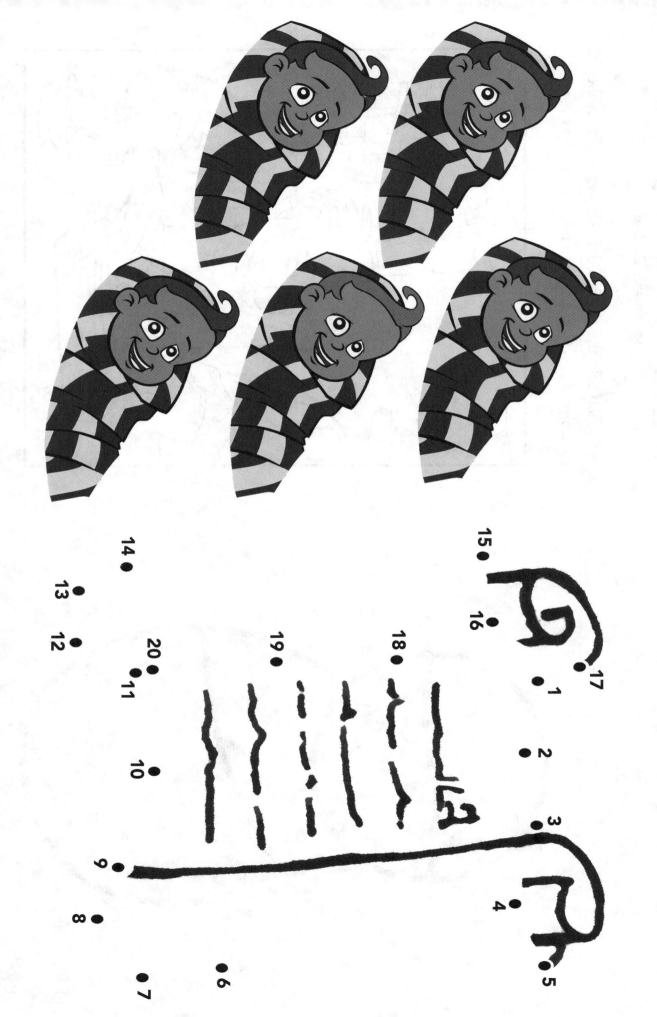

Jeremiah wrote on scrolls. Connect the dots to see what a scroll looks like.

Self-control

Daniel 1:1-21

Daniel and his friends obeyed God, even when the king wanted them to break God's rules.

To be faithful, Daniel had to say no to eating the king's food. Draw something you need to say no to.

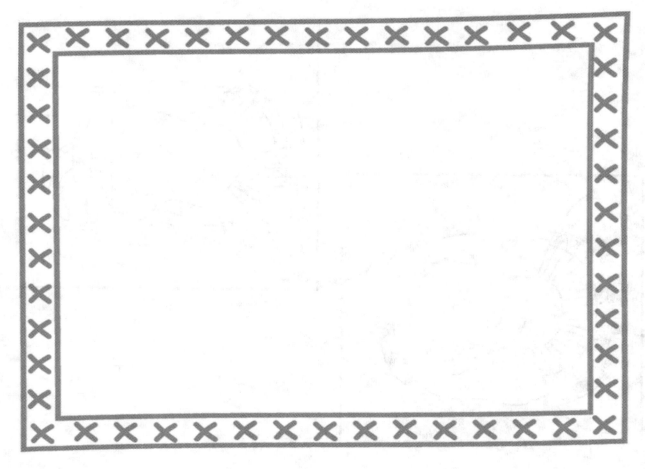

58

Daniel and his friends ate only vegetables for ten days. Circle the vegetables you recognize.

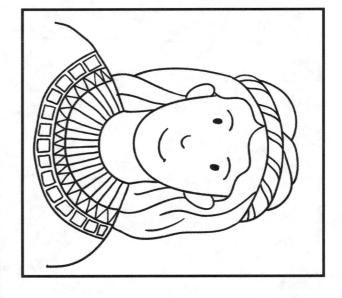

Can you find 5 differences between the pictures of Daniel?

Courageous Friends

Daniel 3:1-30

Three friends made the king angry by refusing to worship anyone other than God. God protected the friends, even when the king tried to kill them!

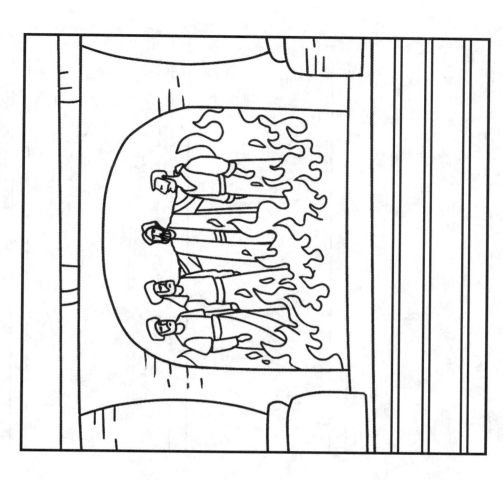

The friends were very brave. You can be brave, too. Draw a picture of a time when you are brave.

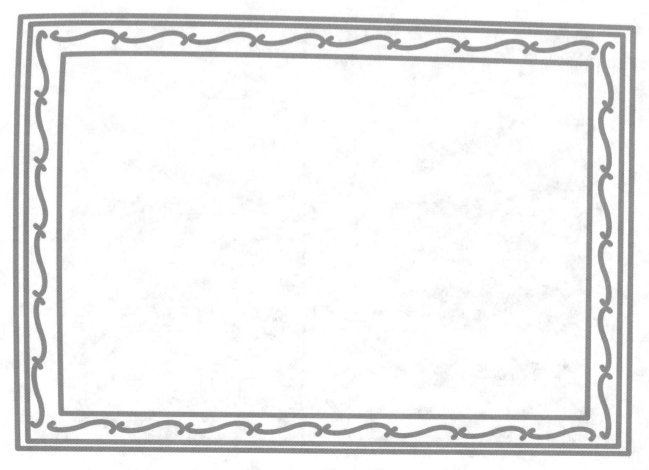

The king saw four people in the fire. Which picture shows the king and the four people?

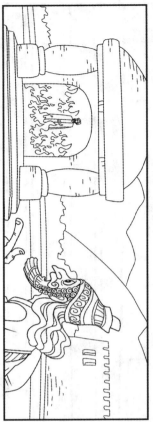
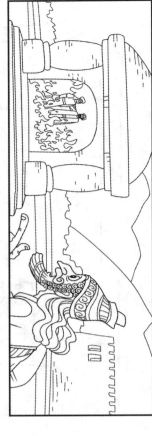
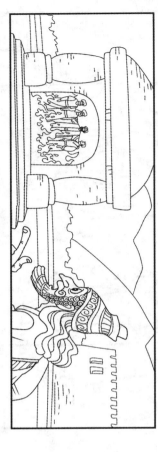
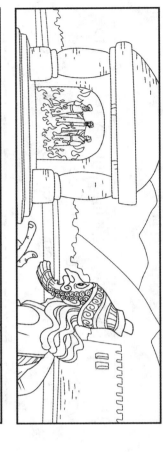

Look for six differences in the two pictures.

Courageous Daniel

Daniel 6:1-28

When Daniel stood up for God, God saved him from the hungry lions!

Even though the lions were hungry, they didn't gobble up Daniel! Give this lion some food to eat.

N	B	O	L
I	O	R	O
A	L	N	V
L	I	E	N
I	N	L	O

To face the lions,
Daniel had to be _____.

Look for the five lions hiding in the lions' den.
Circle them.

DEEP BLUE Jonah and the Fish
Jonah 1–4

Jonah didn't want to do what God told him to do, so he ran away. He ended up being swallowed by a big fish! He prayed to God, and God saved him. Then Jonah chose to obey God.

When Jonah ran away from God he traveled on a boat. Draw a picture of Jonah's boat.

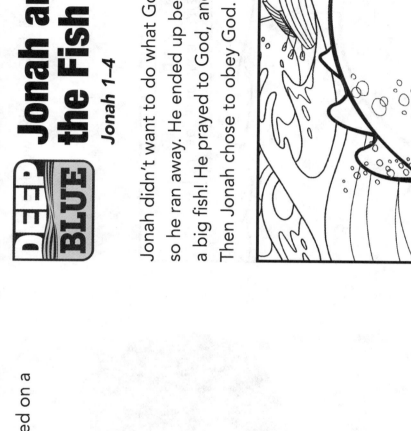

Find the words in the fish. Circle the words and color the picture.

FIND

JONAH FISH GOD SHIP OBEY

```
O B E Y M F E L S
D M S K B I M P H
F V G M J S P M I
Q J O N A H S V P
H A D W L B A Z J
```

Can you put Jonah's story in the right order?

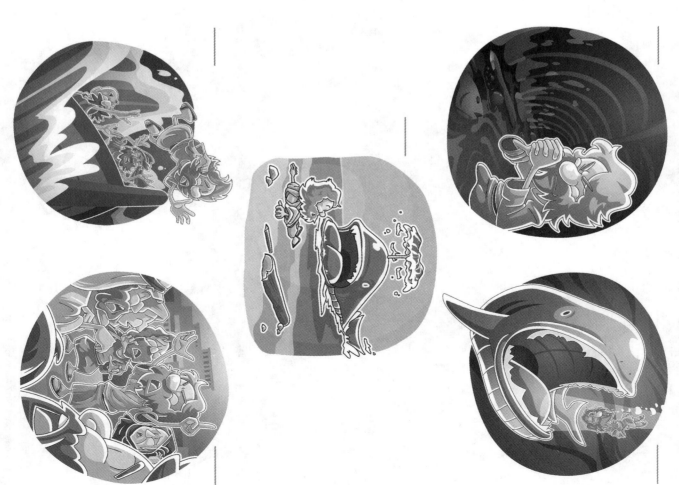
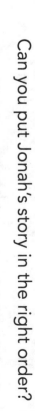

Joseph's Story
Matthew 1:18-24

An angel appeared to Joseph and said, "Joseph, the baby Mary is having is God's gift to the whole world. Marry her. Name the baby Jesus, Emmanuel, which means God with us."

What do you think the angel might have looked like? Draw it in the box below.

How many ways can you find for Joseph to get to Mary?

What was Joseph doing when the angel appeared to him? Place a check mark beside the correct picture.

Follow the Star
Matthew 2:1-12

When Jesus was little, wise men came from far away to worship him. They followed a special star in the sky.

The wise men followed a star all the way to Bethlehem. How many stars can you draw in the frame below?

The wise men brought Jesus three gifts. Add presents to the picture below.

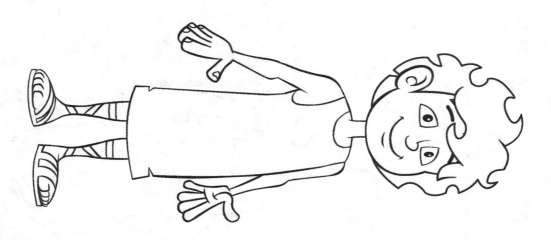

Which wise man looks different from the others? Circle him.

Come to the River

the River

Matthew 3:13-17

Jesus was baptized by John the Baptist. When Jesus came out of the water, a voice from heaven said, "This is my Son. I love him. He makes me happy."

What's your favorite place with water? The beach? A lake? A swimming pool? Draw it below.

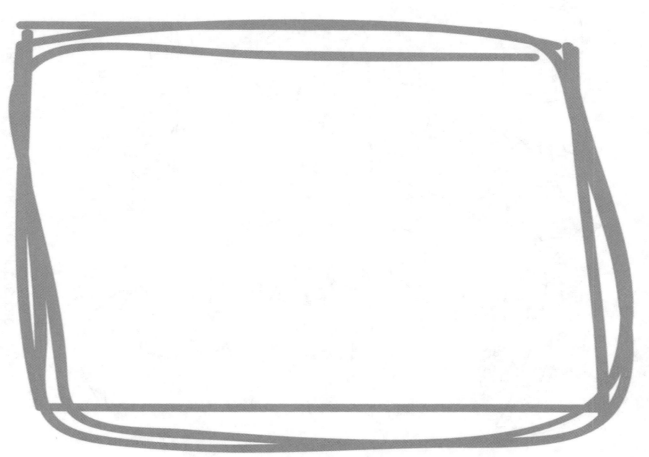

Connect the dots to finish the picture of Jesus' baptism.

The pictures below show children using water for various things, but the water is missing. Add water to each picture and then color the pictures.

DEEP BLUE

Jesus Calls the Fishermen
Matthew 4:18-22

Peter, Andrew, James, and John were fishing when Jesus told them, "Come, follow me." They dropped their fishing nets and followed Jesus!

To follow Jesus, we share love with people and the planet. This makes Jesus happy. Draw a picture of yourself doing something to follow Jesus.

Which set of footprints leads to Jesus?

How many fish are in the net?
Write your answer here. _____

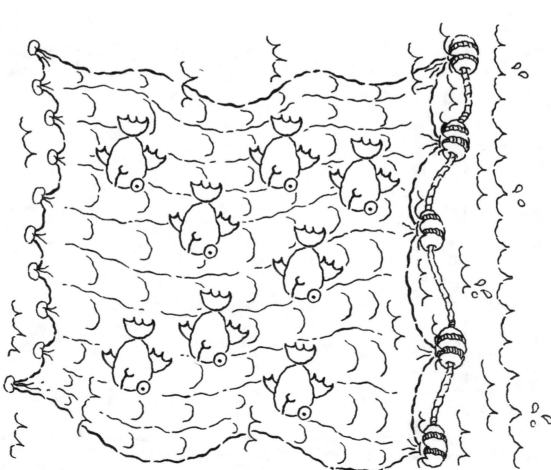

 **Peace**
Matthew 5:1-9

Jesus taught the people that even when we are sad, tired, hurt, grumpy, or grieving, we can have hope that things will get better. We can have peace.

Draw something or someone who makes you feel calm and peaceful.

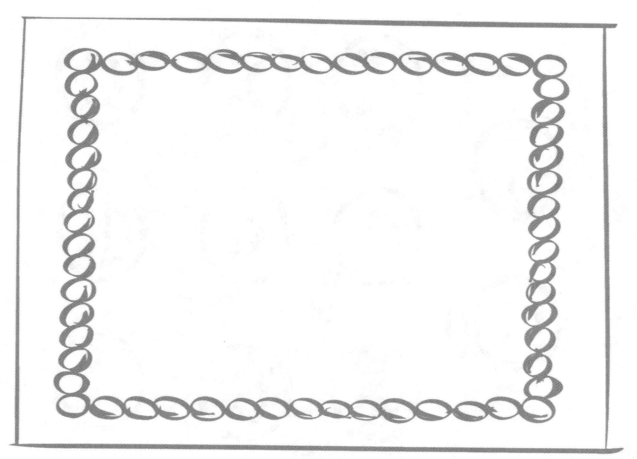

Color the spaces with a dot to see the bird that is a symbol of peace. Trace the dotted letters below.

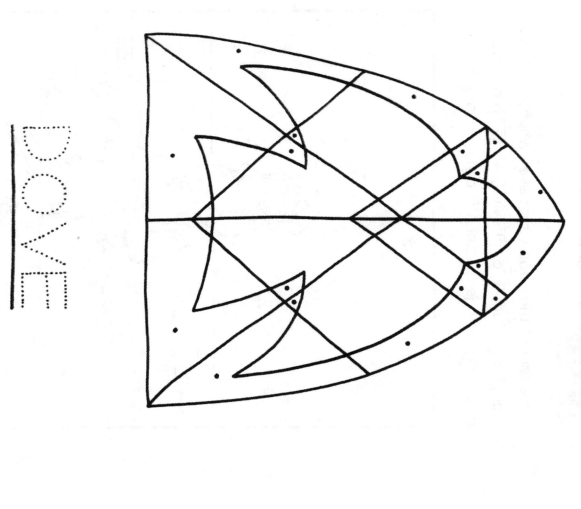

DOVE

Which faces do you think show peace? Draw a square around them.

The Lord's Prayer
Matthew 6:5-15

Jesus taught the people a special prayer: "God in heaven, your name is holy. Let what happens in your kingdom happen on earth. Give us everything we need. Forgive us; help us forgive others. Help us make good choices, instead of bad ones."

In God's kingdom, everyone has everything they need. What do you think God's kingdom looks like? Draw it below.

Sometimes people hold their hands a special way when they pray. Connect the dots to see what this way looks like.

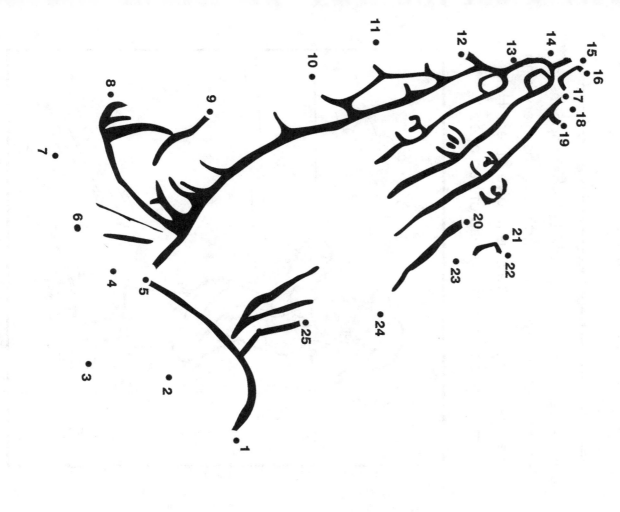

Which pictures show children making good choices? Color those pictures and draw an X through the other pictures.

The Birds of the Air
Matthew 6:25-34

Jesus taught, "Don't worry about the things you need. God will take care of you like God takes care of the birds and the flowers."

God gives us everything we need to live, but not everything we want. Draw three things that you need to live and two things that you want.

68

God helps us find our way. Help the baby birds find the way to their nest.

God gives the flowers sun and rain to help them grow. Add flowers, a sun, and rain to the picture below.

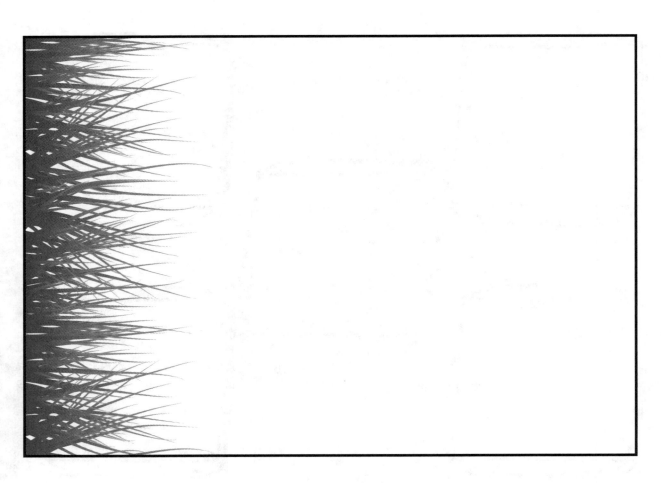

The Golden Rule
Matthew 7:12

Jesus taught, "Treat people in the same way that you want people to treat you."

Draw or write some of your family's rules in the frame below.

Fill in the letter O in the blanks marked with a heart (♥) and the letter T in the blanks marked with a star (★) to complete Jesus' message.

★REA★
PE♥PLE
IN
★HE
SAME WAY
HA★ Y♥U
WAN★
PE♥PLE
★REA★ Y♥U.

Circle the kids who are following the Golden Rule.

The Two Houses

Matthew 7:24-27

To help the people understand that they could trust God, Jesus told a story about two houses. One house was strong, but the other washed away.

What does your home look like? Draw it in the frame below.

Jesus told parables, which are stories that teach us about God. Which picture tells the parable of about the wise builder who built the strong house?

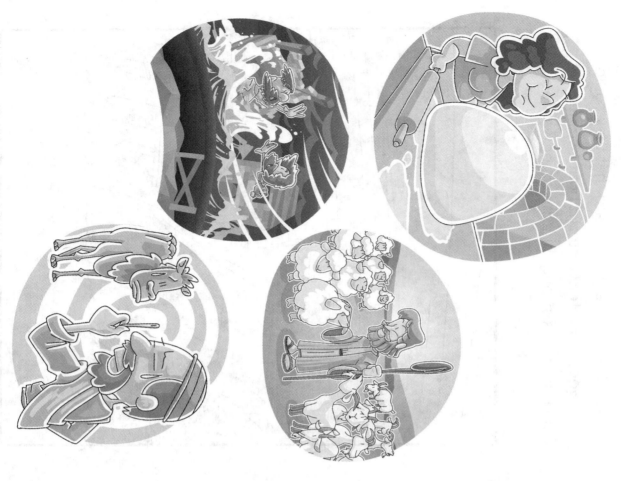

Color the spaces with a dot to see Jesus' message for the people!

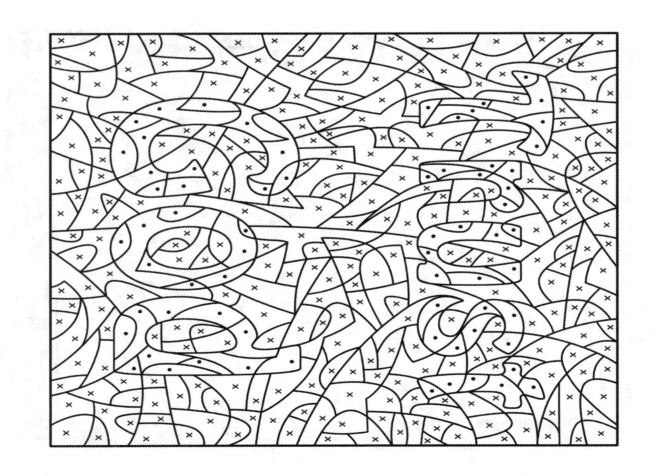

The Man in the Synagogue

DEEP BLUE

Matthew 12:9-14

Jesus healed a man's hurt hand even though it broke some of the Jewish leaders' rules. The man was very happy!

Trace your hand in the frame below. Have you ever hurt your hand? Draw a band aid on the hurt spot.

Jesus went to the synagogue to worship God.
What are some of the ways we worship God?
Circle the ways you worship God in your church.

The leaders were mad at Jesus. Can you find the two leaders that match?

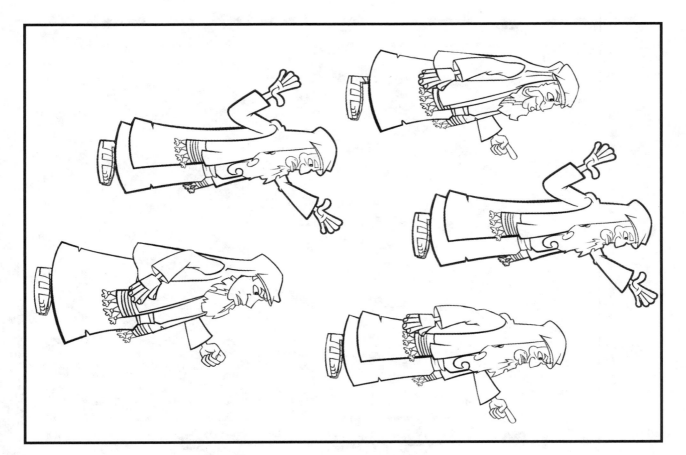

Jesus and the Children

Matthew 19:13-15

Jesus loved being with children. He told his disciples that grown-ups should love God as much as children do.

Draw a picture of Jesus and you. Jesus loves you!

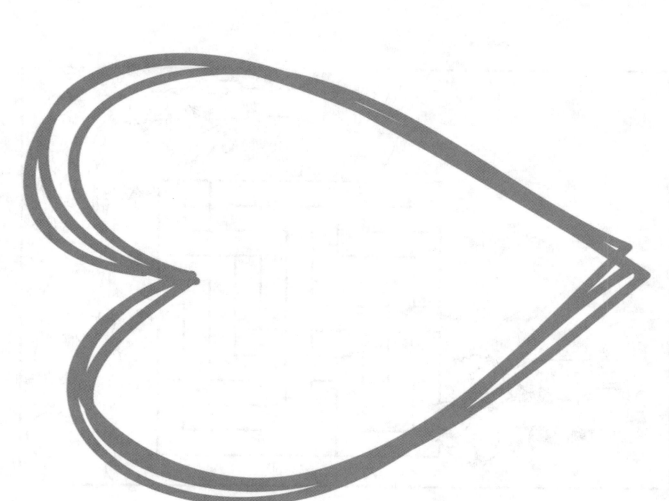

Can you find 5 differences between the two pictures?

Help the children find their way to Jesus.

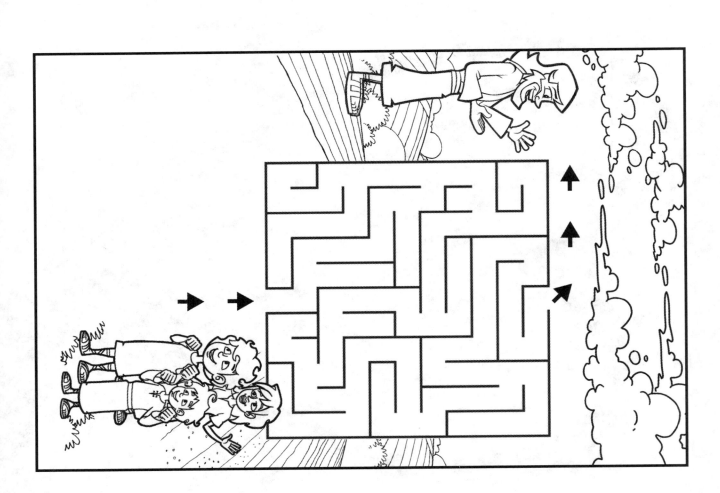

Hosanna!

Matthew 12:1-11

Jesus rode into the city of Jerusalem on a donkey. The people shouted, "Hosanna!" and waved palm branches.

What do you do when you are happy? Maybe you dance or sing or jump? Draw a picture of you celebrating in the frame.

Draw the leaves on the palm branches.

Put the scenes in the order they happened in the story. Draw lines from the numbers to the scenes.

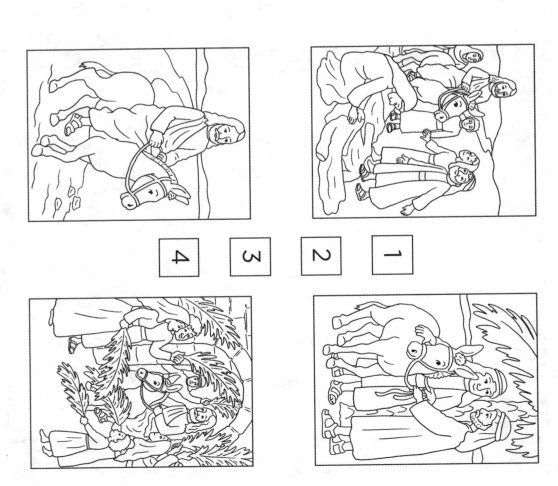

1

2

3

4

At the Last Supper

Matthew 26:17-30

At Jesus' last meal with the disciples, he shared bread and wine with his friends, saying, "Take and eat. This is my body," and, "Drink. This is the cup of the new covenant." This meal reminds us that Jesus loves us very much!

Jesus showed love to his disciples by serving them at the Passover meal. Draw a picture of how you show love.

Circle the six items that don't belong in the picture.

In the Garden
DEEP BLUE
Matthew 26:31-58

Jesus and his closest friends went to a garden to pray. Jesus' friends fell asleep instead of praying. Judas brought people to the garden to arrest Jesus.

Jesus prayed in a garden. Draw a picture of a place you like to pray.

What did the disciples do while Jesus prayed?
Cross out the letters **W - I - T - H** to see the answer.

T	F	W	H
E	T	L	L
H	T	A	I
S	H	W	L
I	T	E	W
I	H	T	P
W	T	P	H

Answer: _____

Finish drawing the olive tree by tracing the dotted line and adding leaves and olives.

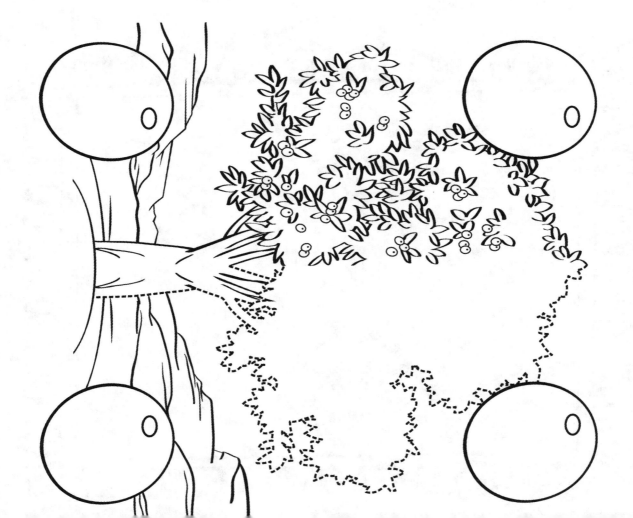

Cock-a-doodle-doo!

Matthew 26:69-75

Jesus had warned Peter that Peter would tell people that he didn't know Jesus before the rooster crowed three times. Jesus was right! Peter denied being Jesus' friend. This made Peter sad.

Draw a picture of a time you've done something wrong. How did it make you feel?

Match the rooster to his shadow.

Circle the three hidden roosters in the picture.

Alleluia!

Matthew 28:1-10

When Mary and Mary Magdalene went to Jesus' tomb three days after he died, it was empty! Jesus was gone! An angel told them to tell the disciples. Then the women saw Jesus, alive again! Alleluia!

Jesus told the women not to be afraid. Draw something you are afraid of, then scratch it out. God is with us even when we are scared!

The women found Jesus's tomb empty. An angel said to them, "He is not here; he has risen!" Connect the dots to see what the angel was sitting on.

Mary and Mary Magdalene were surprised, scared, and happy when they saw the empty tomb. Color the faces that show how the women might have felt.

The Great Commission

DEEP BLUE

Matthew 28:16-20

Jesus taught his disciples one last time, saying, "Go to all people and teach them about me and to love one another. I will be with you always, wherever you go, for all time."

Jesus told the disciples to tell people all over the world that God loves them. Add people all over this picture of the earth.

Jesus showed the disciples how to tell people about him. Help the disciples find their way to spread God's love.

We can tell people about Jesus' love through our words and our actions. These kids are showing love. Pick one of these ways that you can share love. Color its picture and ask God to help you do it this week.

 **DEEP BLUE**

A Voice in the Wilderness

Mark 1:9-11

Jesus was baptized by John the Baptizer. When Jesus came up out of the water, a voice from heaven said, "You are my Son. I love you. You make me happy."

Have you ever seen someone being baptized in your church? Draw a picture of what you remember or how you imagine it would be.

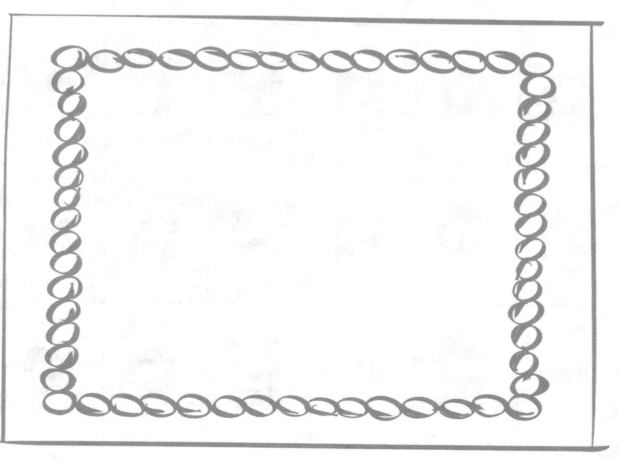

Circle the picture that shows Jesus being baptized.

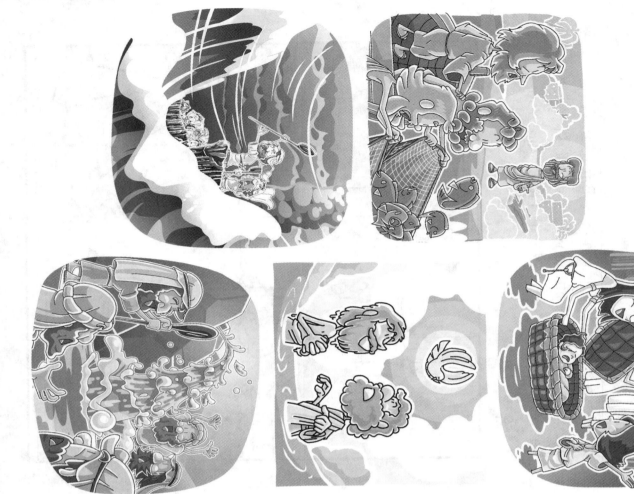

What did God say when Jesus was baptized? Draw an X over every other letter to see.

X̶	I	S
L	K	O
B	V	M
E	T	Y
Q	O	W
U	Z	!

The Four Friends

Mark 2:1-12

Four friends brought their friend who was paralyzed to Jesus. Jesus said, "Get up and walk!" The man picked up his mat and walked. Everyone was amazed and praised God!

In order to get their friend to Jesus, the four friends had to lower him down through the ceiling. How silly! Draw a picture of something silly.

Help the four friends get their sick friend to Jesus.

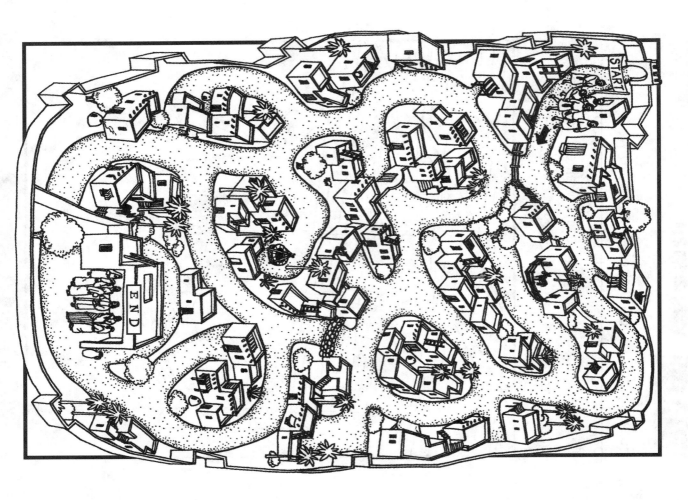

The man's friends helped him by bringing him to Jesus. Circle the things you can do to help others. Can you think of other ways to help?

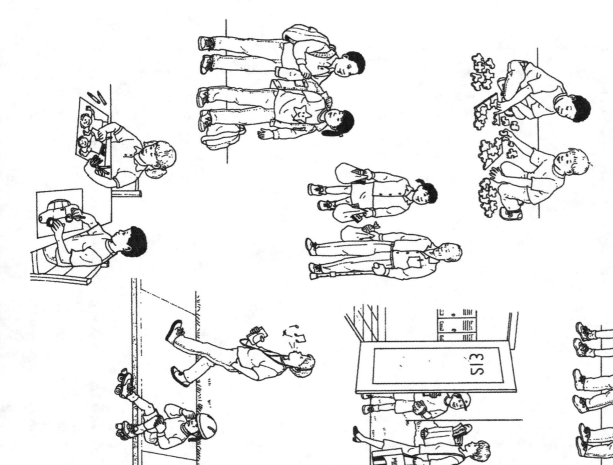

Jesus Calms the Storm

Mark 4:35-41

Jesus and his disciples were in a boat in the middle of a big storm. The disciples were so scared that they thought they were going to die! Jesus told the wind to be silent and still, and everything was calm.

The disciples were very scared. Draw a picture of something that makes you scared. Then draw a heart around it to remind you that Jesus is always with you, even when you are scared.

While the disciples were scared, Jesus was sleeping peacefully. Which picture shows Jesus in the storm?

Connect the dots to see what the boat might have looked like.

Jairus's Daughter

Mark 5:21-24, 35-43

A little girl was very sick, so sick that her parents thought she was dead. Jesus took the little girl's hand and said, "Get up!" Jesus made her alive again, and she stood up!

Have you ever known a child who was very sick? Draw a get-well card as a prayer for kids who are sick.

82

What did Jesus tell Jairus to do? Circle every third
letter and write them in the blanks to find out.

– – – – – – – –

C	E	T	K
O	R	Q	N
U	P	U	S
A	J	T	I

Help Jesus find his way to the sick little girl.

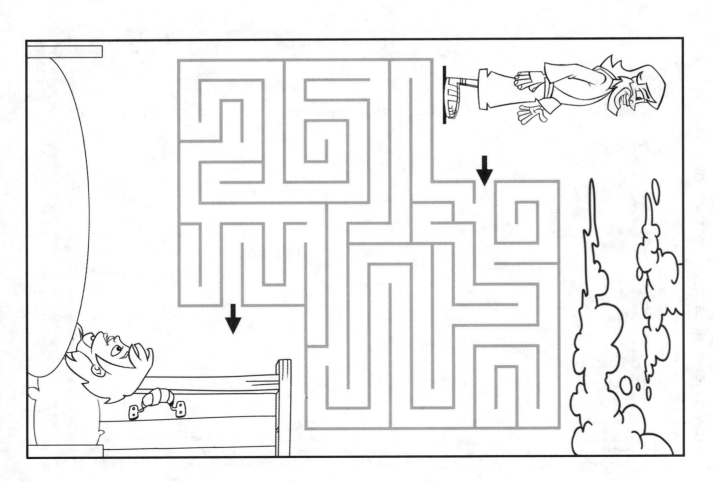

Go Two by Two

Mark 6:7-13

Jesus sent his friends, the disciples, to teach and to heal people throughout the villages. Each friend took a buddy!

It's good to have a buddy! Draw a picture of you with a friend.

Can you spot five differences between the pictures?

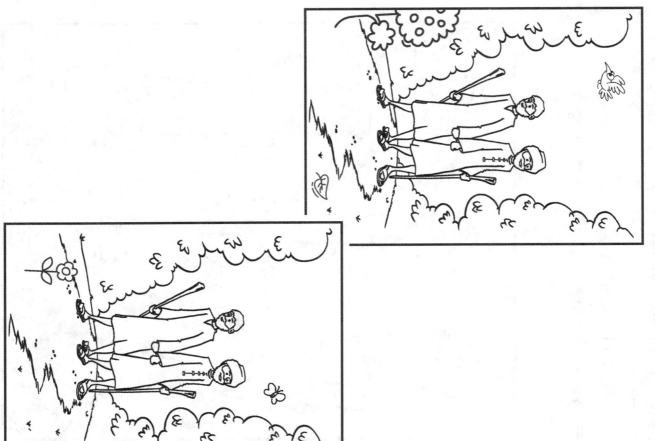

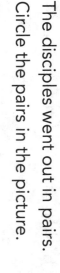

The disciples went out in pairs.
Circle the pairs in the picture.

Bartimaeus Shouts to Jesus

Mark 10:46-52

Bartimaeus was blind. He asked Jesus to heal his eyes, so Jesus did! Bartimaeus could see! He became one of Jesus' followers.

Bartimaeus was excited to be able to see! Draw something you like to look at.

Bartimaeus was blind. What part of his body did he ask Jesus to heal?

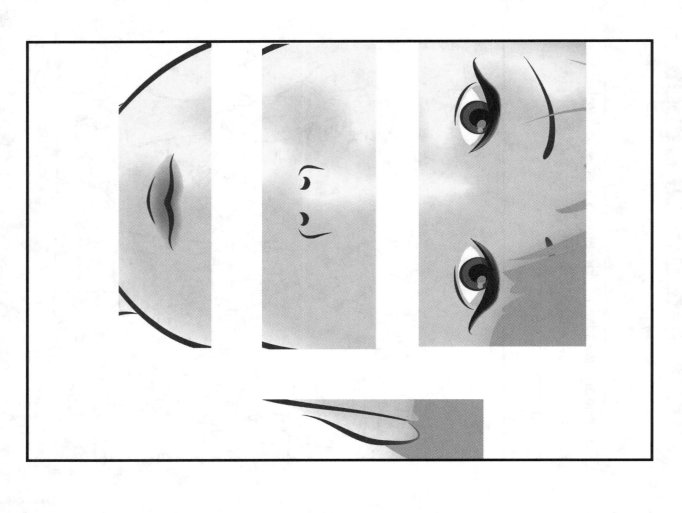

Once Bartimaeus was healed, he followed Jesus. Trace the line that leads him to Jesus.

DEEP BLUE

People Welcome Jesus

Mark 11:1-11

Jesus' friends found a donkey for him to ride into the city of Jerusalem. The people cheered for Jesus and waved palm branches. It was like a parade!

Jesus rode a donkey. What animal would you choose to ride? Draw it in the frame below.

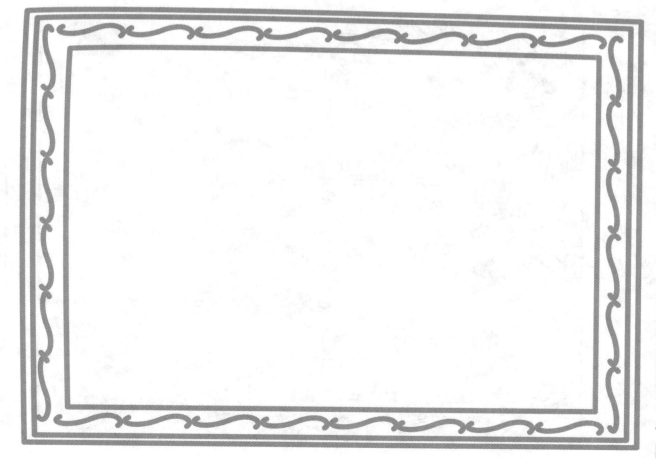

Can you find the right road to Jerusalem?

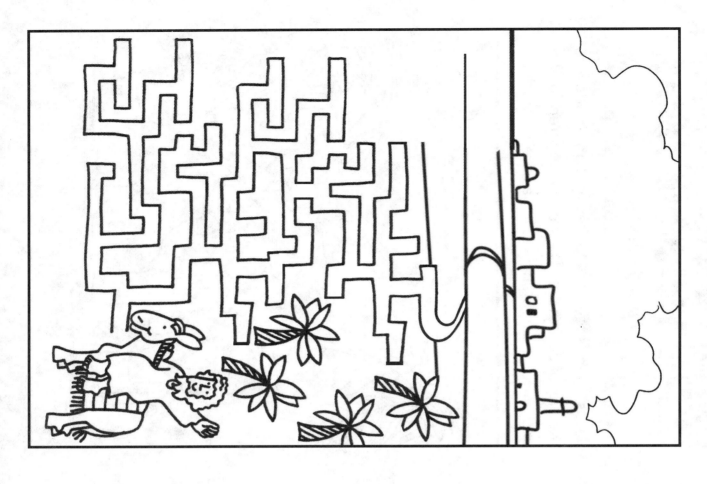

Count the palm branches. How many do you see?

Jesus Breaks the Bread

Mark 14:12-26

Jesus had one last meal with his disciples. During the meal, Jesus took the bread, blessed it, broke it, and gave it to his friends. Jesus took the cup, gave thanks, and gave it to his friends. He reminded his friends that he loved them very much.

Jesus told his followers to remember him by having this meal. We call it communion or the Lord's Supper. Draw a picture of communion at your church.

Jesus shared bread with his disciples, but there is no bread in the picture below! Add the bread.

Connect the dots to see what the grapes and wheat become.

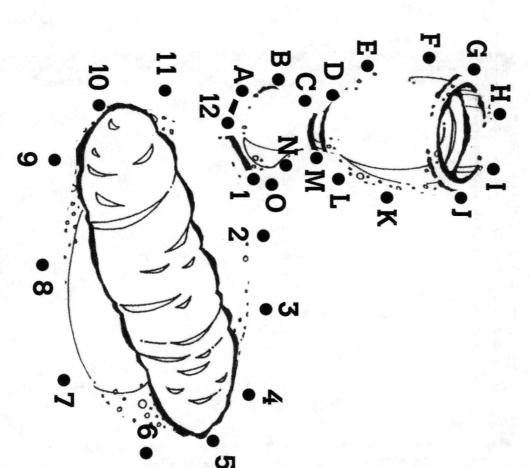

DEEP BLUE Elizabeth and Zechariah

Luke 1:5-25

Elizabeth and Zechariah were very, very old. They didn't think they would get to have a baby. God gave them a special baby named John.

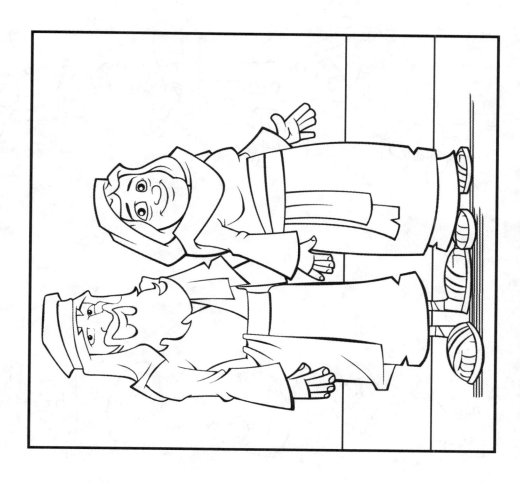

Elizabeth and Zechariah didn't think they would ever have a baby, but God gave them John. What is a gift God has given you?

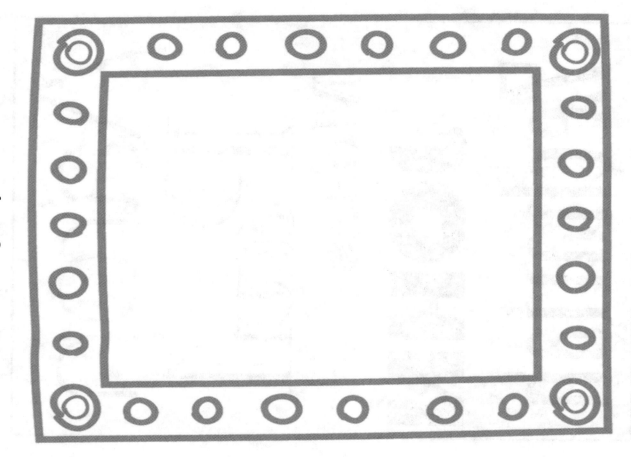

In the Temple, people worshiped God in many of the ways we do: they prayed, read scripture, sang, gave an offering, and had a lesson. Draw lines to connect the pictures of each part of worship then to pictures of how we worship now.

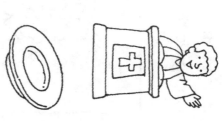

The angel told Zechariah to call the baby a name that starts with J. Circle the name below.

Aaron

Paul

Moses

JOHN

Zechariah

DEEP BLUE

Gabriel's Message

Luke 1:26-38

And angel, Gabriel, visited Mary. He told her that God was going to give Mary a baby that was God's own son! She was to name him Jesus. Mary said, "I will do what God wants me to do."

Mary said, "I will do what God wants me to do." What do you think God wants you to do? Draw yourself doing that thing in the frame below.

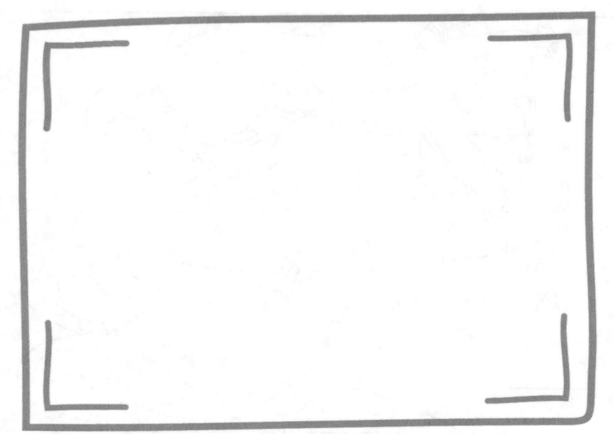

Help the angel find
his way to Mary.

Connect the lines to complete the picture.

Mary Visits Elizabeth

Luke 1:39-66

Mary visited her cousin, Elizabeth. God was giving both of them special babies to take care of. They could tell already that the babies, John and Jesus, would be important to each other.

Draw someone who is special to you.

Elizabeth and Mary were very happy to see each other. Draw their faces in the picture below.

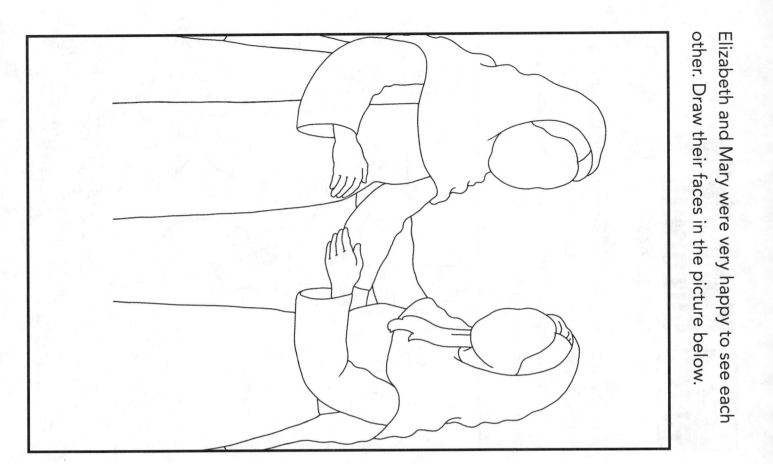

Help Mary find her way to Elizabeth.

Start

Jesus Is Born

Luke 2:1-7

Mary and Joseph traveled to Bethlehem. The town was so full that they had to sleep with the animals. That night, Jesus was born! Mary wrapped him up and laid him in a manger.

It's Jesus' birthday! Draw Jesus a birthday party.

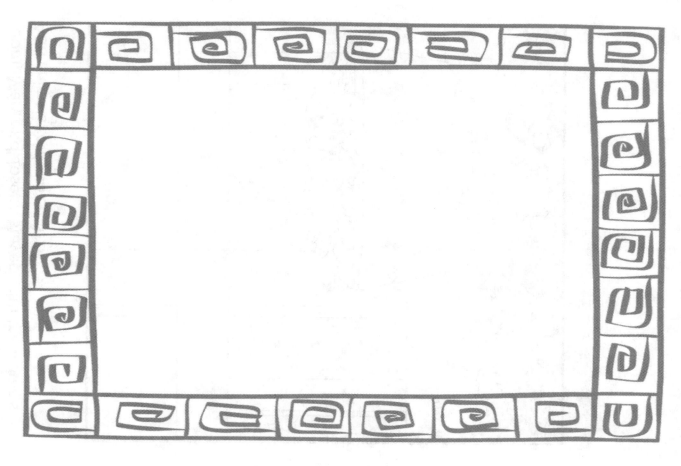

Connect the dots to see Jesus and his family.

Because there wasn't room for them in the guest room, Mary and Joseph stayed with the animals. Add animals to the picture.

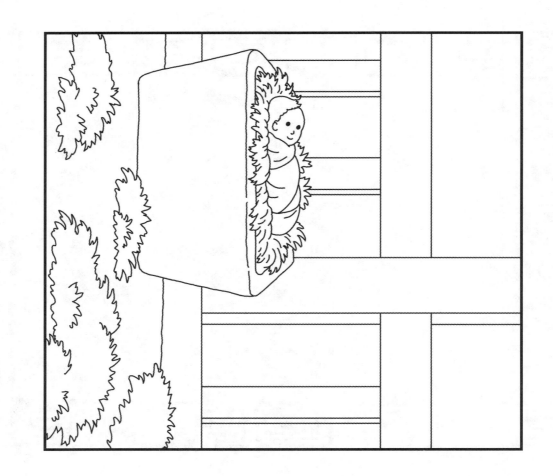

Joyous News

Luke 2:8-20

An angel appeared to shepherds near Bethlehem and told them that God's son had been born. They hurried to Bethlehem to see baby Jesus!

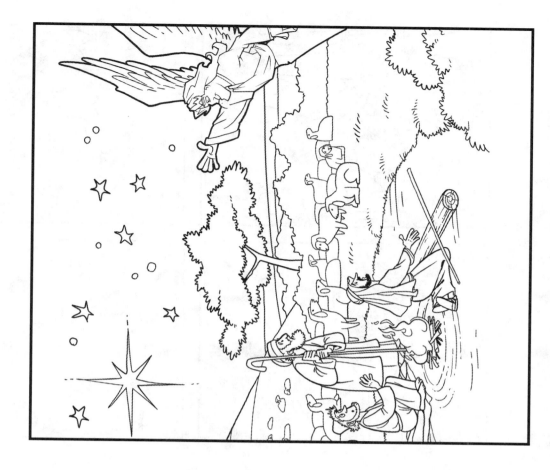

The shepherds were in a hurry to see baby Jesus. Draw yourself running towards Jesus.

91

Number the pictures on the correct order.

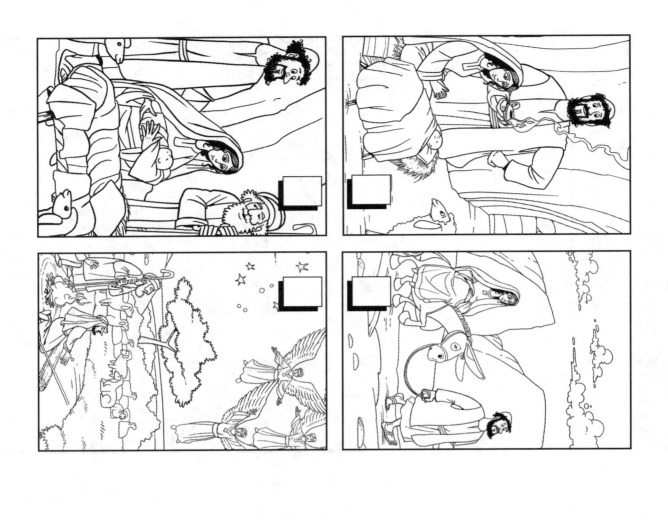

Help the shepherds find their way to baby Jesus, and then help them find their way home and share the good news on the way.

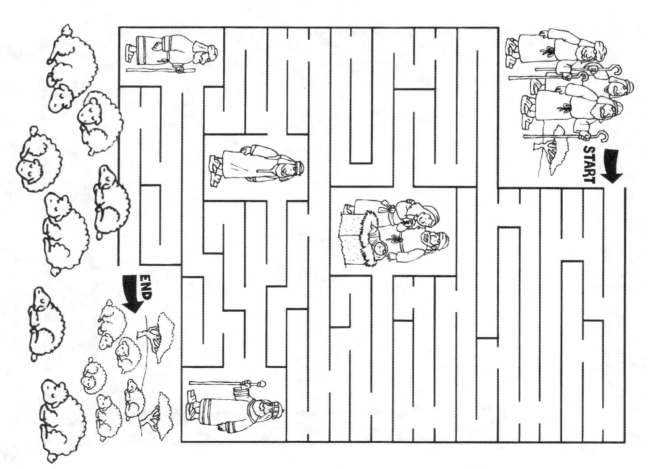

START

END

Simeon and Anna

Luke 2:25-38

Simeon and Anna were prophets who stayed in the Temple. When Mary and Joseph brought Jesus to the Temple, Anna and Simeon recognized him as the Messiah and praised God.

Simeon waited a long time to see the Messiah. What's something that you have waited a long time for? Draw it in the frame.

Help Anna and Simeon find baby Jesus in the Temple.

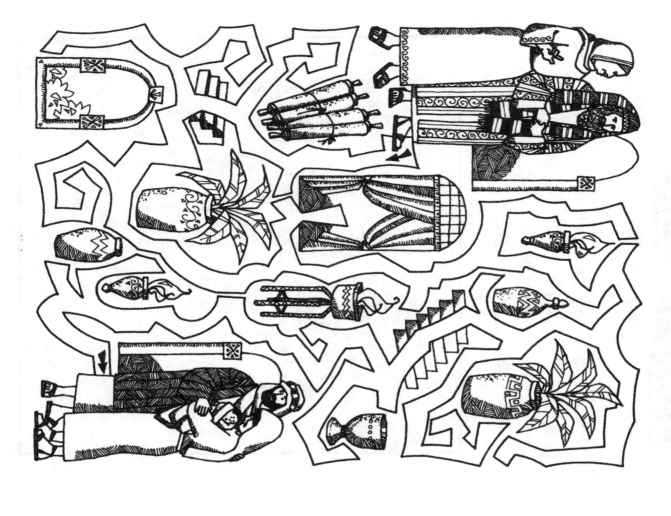

Can you find 5 differences between the two pictures of Anna?

DEEP BLUE

Talk with the Teachers

Luke 2:39-52

When Jesus was a boy, he got separated from his parents. It turned out that Jesus was still in the Temple, talking to the church leaders. He already understood so much about God!

Who is your favorite teacher? Draw him or her below.

Put the events in order by drawing a line from each
number to the correct picture.

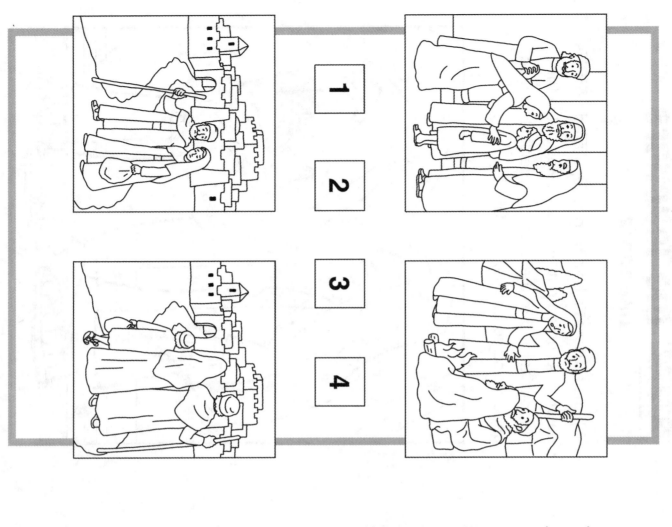

1	2

3	4

Can you find Jesus
among the elders?

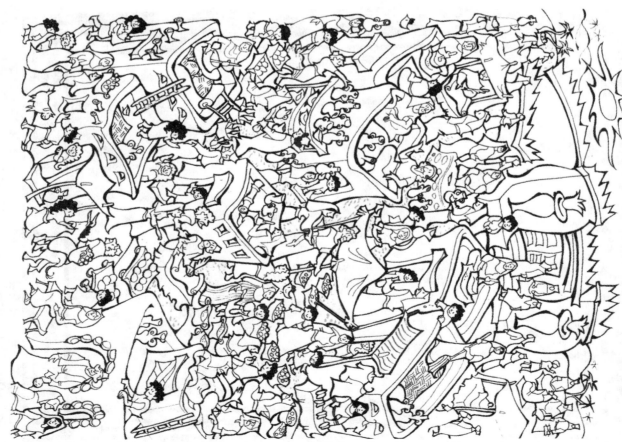

Jesus

DEEP BLUE

Jesus Is Baptized
Luke 3:1-22

Jesus went to see John, who was at the river teaching people about God. Jesus asked John to baptize him. When John baptized Jesus, a dove flew down, and God's voice said, "You are my son, whom I dearly love."

John wore animal furs and ate bugs. Draw bugs all over this page!

John baptized many people and Jesus. Number the pictures in order. Write an X beside the picture that didn't happen.

When Jesus was baptized, the Holy Spirit appeared in what form? Connect the dots to see.

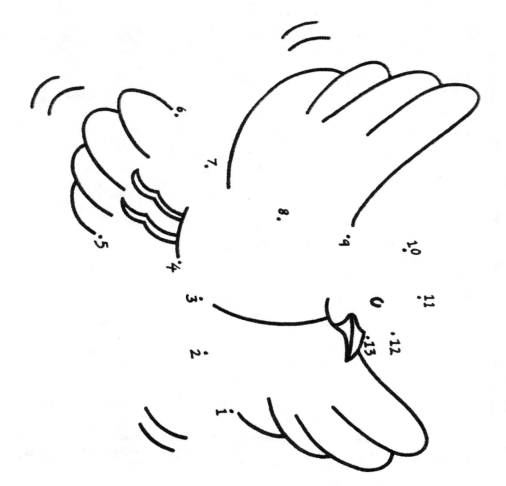

DEEP BLUE Jesus Chooses
Luke 4:1-13

Even when things were difficult, Jesus chose to follow God's rules for his life.

Draw a picture of a time when you made a bad choice. Then draw hearts all over it to remind you that God loves you anyway!

Connect the dots to see how many days Jesus fasted in the wilderness.

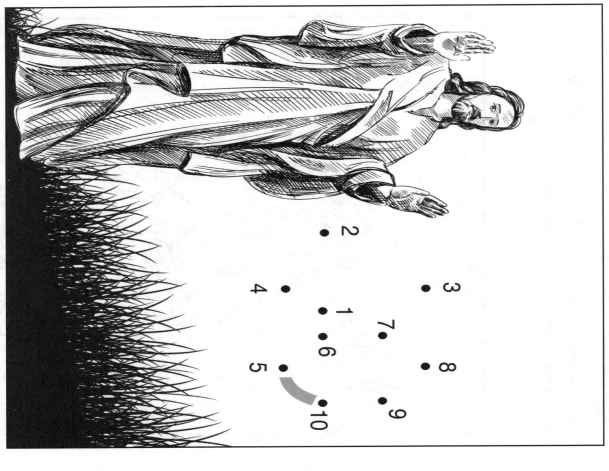

Circle the kids who are making good choices.

Jesus Brings Good News

Luke 4:14-30

One day in worship, Jesus read Scripture that told everyone that he was the Messiah. The people were angry and confused because they thought he was just Jesus, Mary and Joseph's son. They did not know that Jesus was God's son!

Jesus read scripture from a scroll. Now we read Bibles instead of scrolls. Draw a Bible.

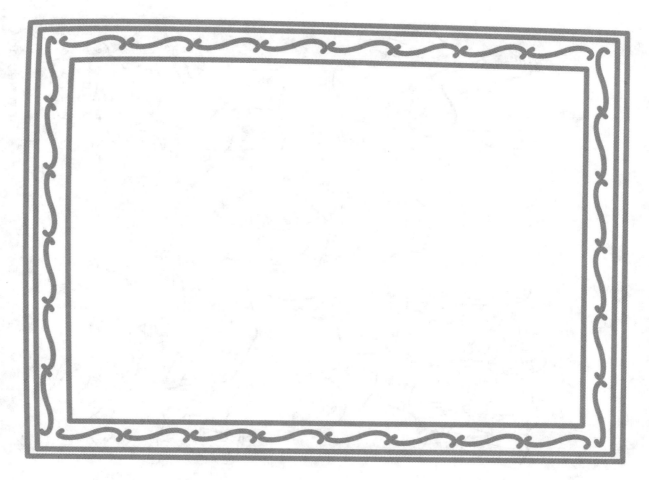

96

Find the scrolls in the picture below.

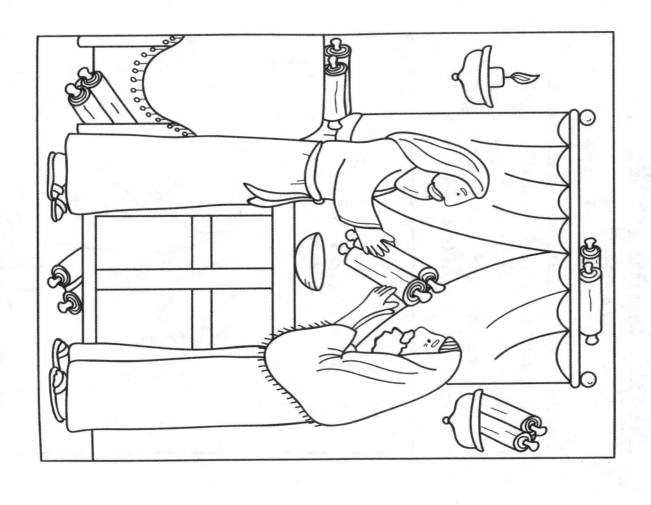

You can help spread the good news of God's love, too. Circle and color the pictures that show what you can do.

Jesus Heals

Luke 4:38-44

Peter's mother-in-law was very sick. She had a fever. Jesus healed her!

Draw a picture of yourself praying for someone you know.

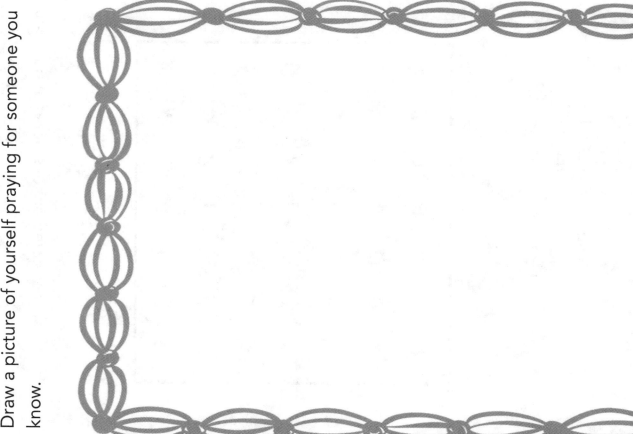

Circle the items that don't belong in the mother-in-law's bedroom.

Computer
Soccer ball

Television
Light switch
Fan

Candy bar
Roller skates

Jesus visited Peter's mother-in-law in order to heal her. Find the words in the puzzle below.

H	M	N	S	I	C	K
E	O	P	T	W	P	G
A	T	R	J	R	L	P
L	H	A	E	Y	Z	E
A	E	Y	S	X	T	E
X	R	X	U	Q	D	R
K	Z	B	S	U	U	R

JESUS   HEAL
PETER   SICK
MOTHER   PRAY

DEEP BLUE

Jesus Calls Levi

Luke 5:27-32

People didn't like tax collectors. Levi was a tax collector, and Jesus spent time with him anyway. Some of the leaders didn't like this. But Jesus loved Levi anyway!

Even though we all make bad choices sometimes, God still loves us! Draw balloons and party decorations to celebrate God's love.

Jesus invited Levi to a dinner. What's missing in the picture below? Draw it in.

Levi took money from the people. How many coins can you find in this picture?

The Two Debtors

Luke 7:41-43

Jesus told a story about how God forgives everyone, no matter what or how much they have done wrong.

The people in Jesus' story were very thankful to God. Draw something or someone you are thankful for.

Jesus told this story because a woman gave him a special gift. Fill in the letters that match the shapes below to see her message to Jesus.

★ = H   ♥ = K

■ = N   ▼ = T   ● = Y

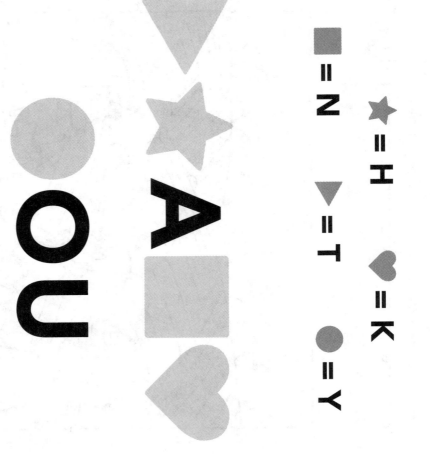

Connect the dots to see what the men in Jesus' story owed the money-lender.

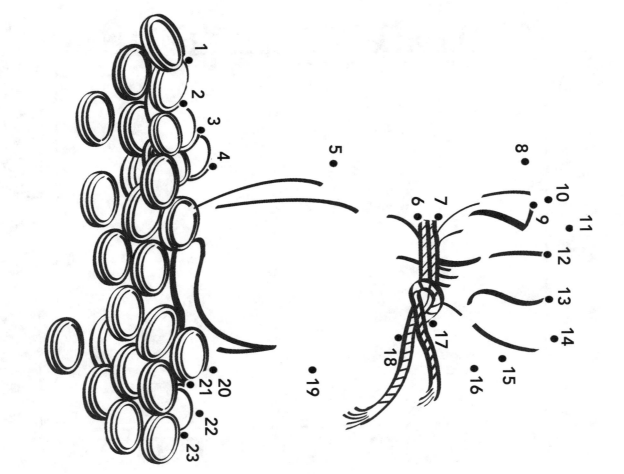

Women Follow Jesus

Luke 8:1-3

Even though we hear a lot about Jesus' twelve disciples who were men, he also had disciples who were women, like Mary Magdelene, Joanna, and Susanna.

Who is a woman you know who follows Jesus? Draw her in the frame below.

Which path will lead the women to Jesus?

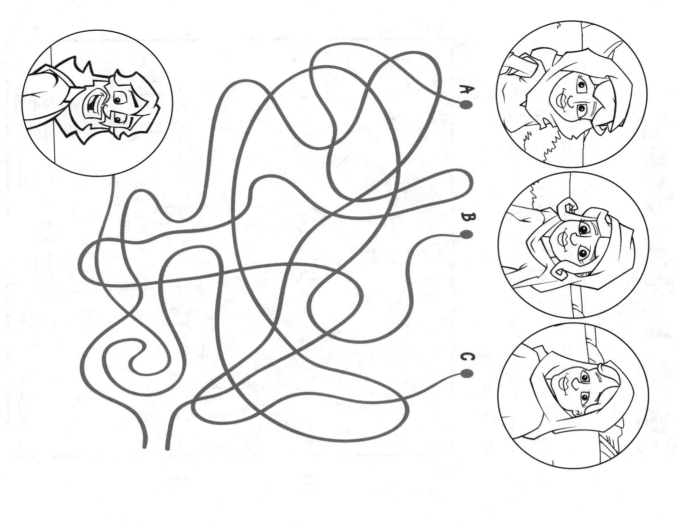

The women followed Jesus as he traveled, but they also followed Jesus' teachings. Circle the ways you can follow Jesus.

The Sower

Luke 8:4-15

Jesus told a story about a farmer planting seeds. The seeds that were planted in the best soil grew the biggest and healthiest. When we hear God's story, we want it to grow in our hearts like those plants!

Jesus told a story about growing plants. Draw a garden in the frame below.

Draw lines to connect the plants that are alike.

Connect the dots to see how God helps the plants grow!

The Good Samaritan

Luke 10:25-37

Jesus told a story: A man was traveling and got attacked by robbers. He needed help! Two people walked right by without helping. A third person walked by and helped the man. He treated the man like they were neighbors, just like Jesus wanted.

Draw of picture of a time somebody helped you.

Look at the first picture of the Samaritan helping the injured man. Then circle six things that are different in the second picture.

Put the scenes in order. Fill in the correct number at the bottom of each picture.

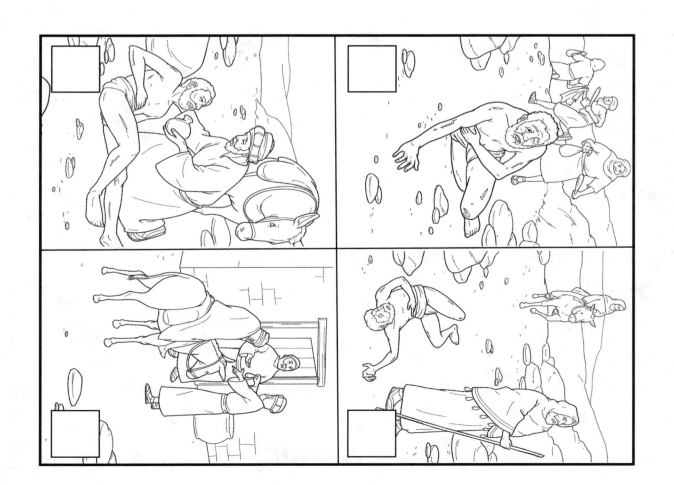

Mary and Martha
Luke 10:38-42

Jesus and his disciples visited two sisters, Mary and Martha. Martha got everything ready for them while Mary sat and listened to Jesus. This made Martha mad, but Jesus reminded her that it's good to be close to Jesus and learn about God.

Mary was still while Martha was busy.
Draw both Mary and Martha in the frame.

Connect the dots to see Martha working hard.

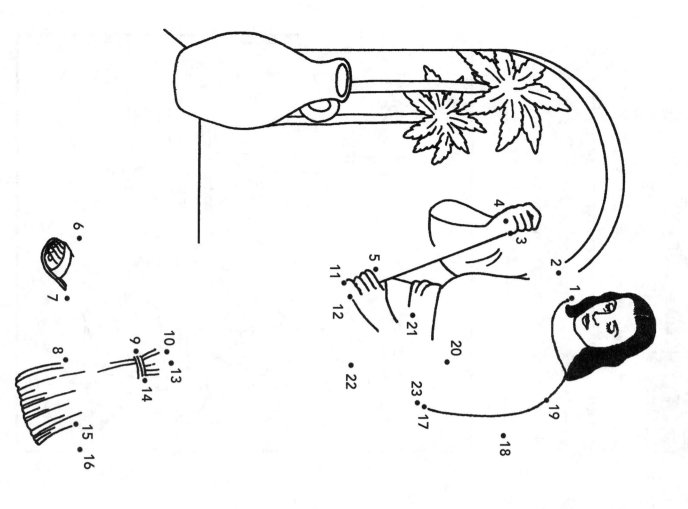

Can you spot 6 differences between the pictures?

The Mustard Seed & the Yeast

Luke 13:18-21

Jesus told a story to teach that even little kindnesses and love can grow into great big things in God's kingdom.

Jesus' story tells us that little things can make a big difference, just like small kids can make a big difference. Draw something you can do to make the world a better place.

Yeast is a powder that you add to dough to make bread. Use a + and = to complete the equation.

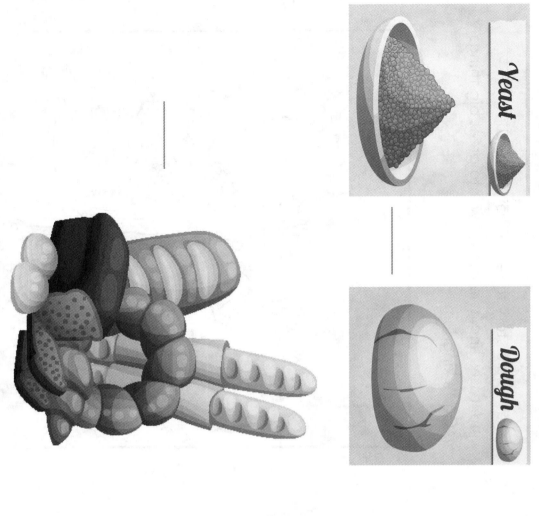

Jesus talked about a mustard seed because a teeny tiny seed can grow into an enormous tree. Here's the seed; you draw the tree.

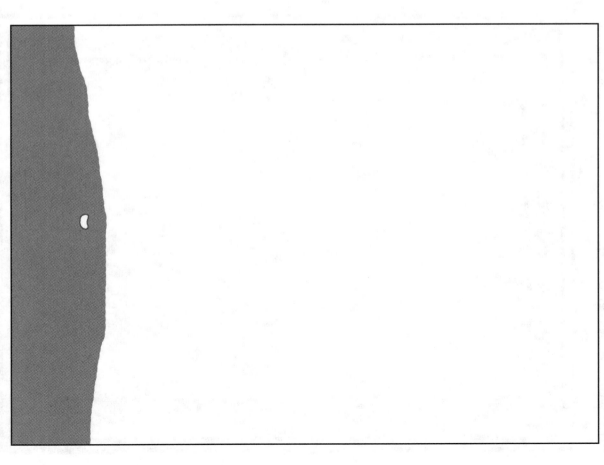

The Stories of the Lost

Luke 15:3-10

Jesus told a story: A shepherd had 100 sheep but one was missing. A woman had ten silver coins but lost one. They searched for the missing items because every single one was important to them. Every single person is important to God!

What is something that is very special to you? Draw it in the frame below.

Put the scenes in order. Fill in the correct number on each picture.

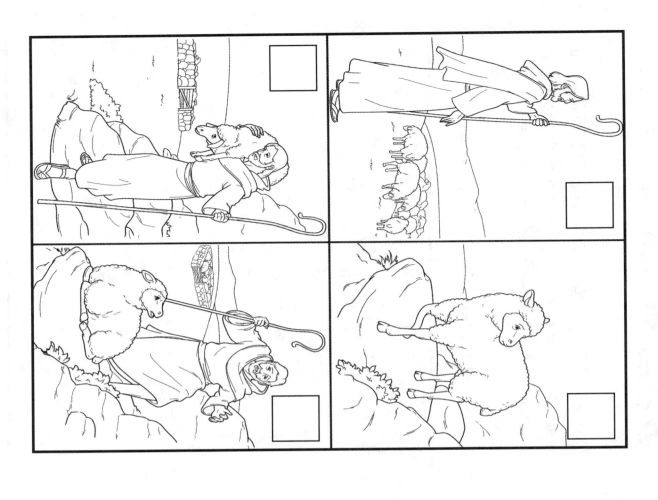

Look for the coin hidden in the flock of sheep.

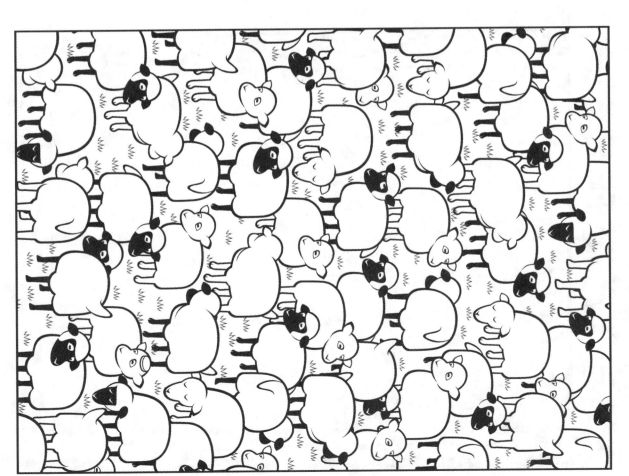

DEEP BLUE
The Forgiving Father
Luke 15:11-32

Jesus told a story: A father had two sons. The younger son ran away. The other son stayed and helped the father. When the younger son came home, the father forgave him and loved him. The older son got grumpy and angry. The father forgave him and loved him, too.

Is there someone you are mad at? Draw them in the frame below. Then ask God to help you forgive them.

Help the son find his way home.

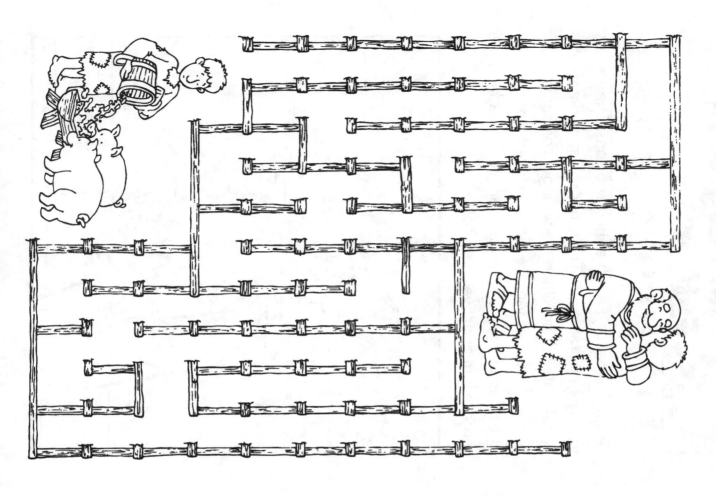

Put the scenes in order. Fill in the correct number in each box.

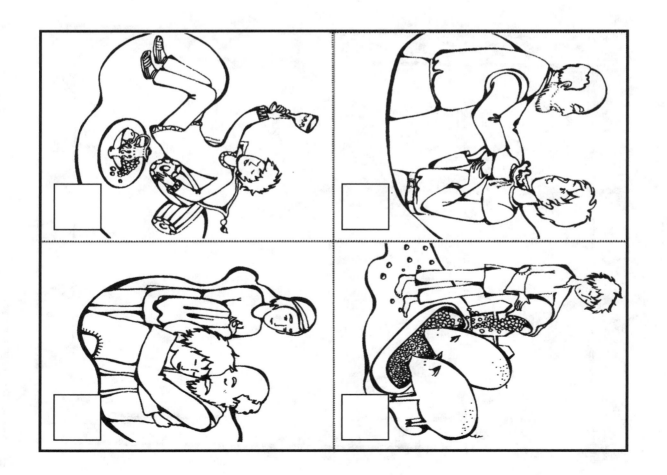

Ten Lepers

Luke 17:11-19

When Jesus was traveling, he came across ten sick men. He cured all the men, but only one man came back to say thank you.

Draw a thank you picture and give it to someone who has helped you.

Connect the letters to follow the path of the men Jesus healed. Connect the numbers to follow the path only one of them took.

Only 1 out of 10 men thanked Jesus for healing him. Circle 1 man and cross out 9.

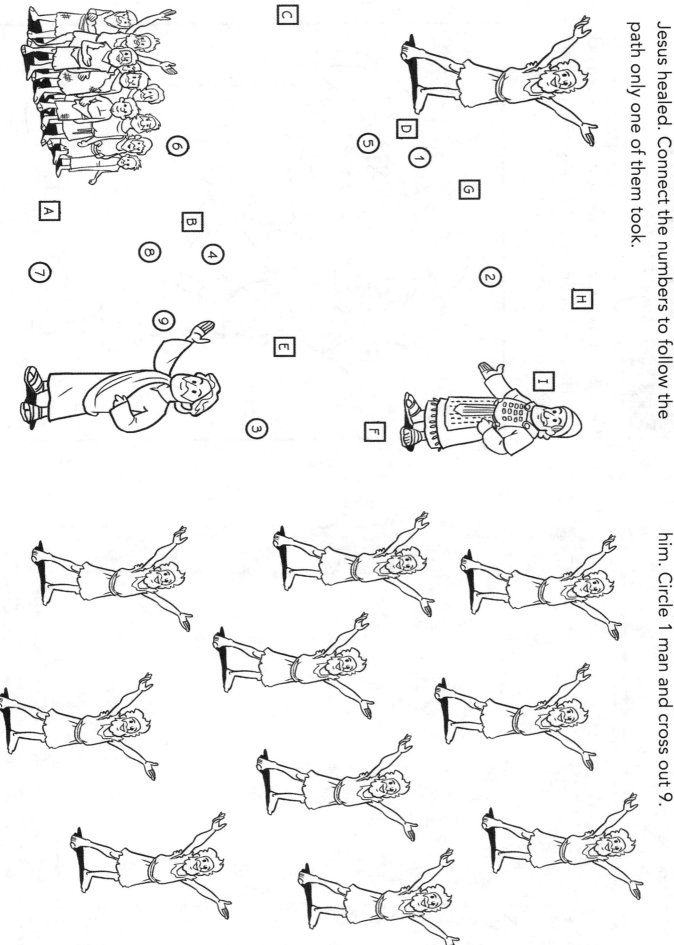

DEEP BLUE

Patience
Luke 18:1-8

Jesus told a story about a woman who had to wait a long time for a judge to help her. God will help us, but sometimes we have to be patient!

Draw a picture of something you had to wait a very long time for.

Can you spot 8 differences between the two pictures?

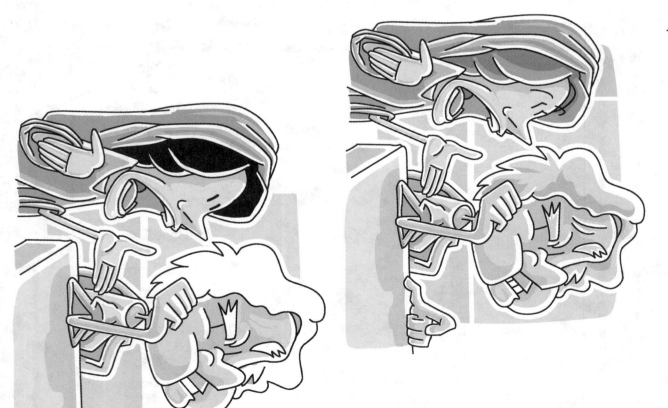

Patience means waiting calmly without trying to hurry things along. These kids worked together to plant a seed and waited patiently for it to grow. Draw in the plant.

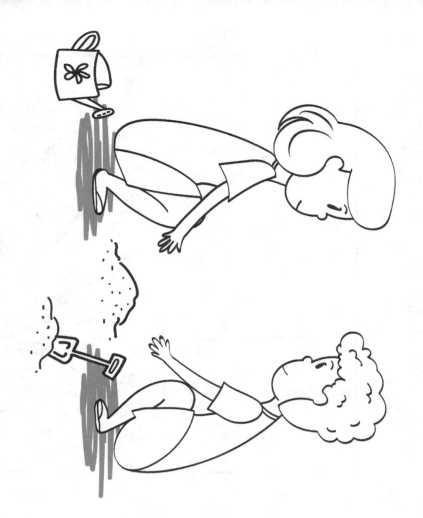

DEEP BLUE The Pharisee & the Tax Collector

Luke 18:9-14

Jesus told a story about two people who prayed in different ways. "God loves us all. No one is better than anyone else," he told the people.

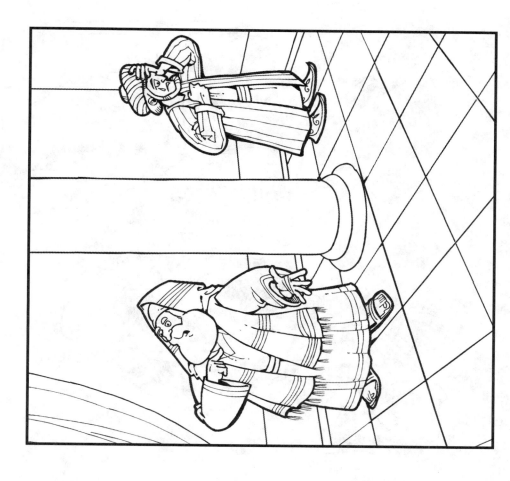

The Pharisee and the tax collector prayed in different ways. How do you pray? Draw a picture of yourself praying.

The Pharisee prayed very loudly, with his head and hands up. The tax collector prayed quietly with his head bowed. Circle the tax collector and draw a box around the Pharisee.

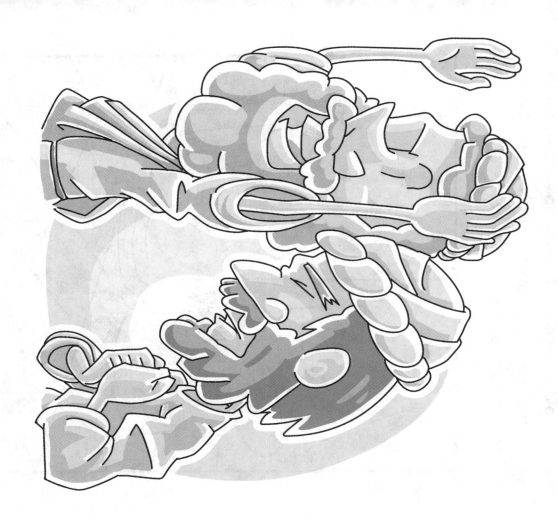

Circle the things you pray for.

Someone who is sick

An ice cream cone

My friends

Someone in a nursing home

A new bike

My mother while she is on a trip

New clothes

A home run

Zacchaeus

Luke 19:1-10

Zacchaeus was a tax collector who cheated people out of their money. Jesus became friends with him anyway. Zacchaeus decided to be fair and generous.

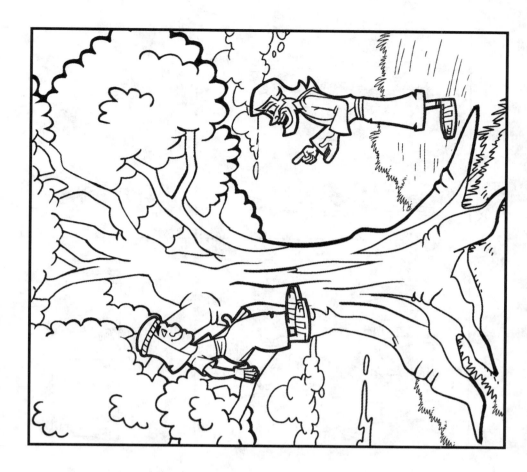

Zacchaeus gave back the money he took unfairly. Draw a picture of Zacchaeus giving his money away.

Zacchaeus wanted to see Jesus, but he was too short to see over the crowd. Circle the shorter item in each picture.

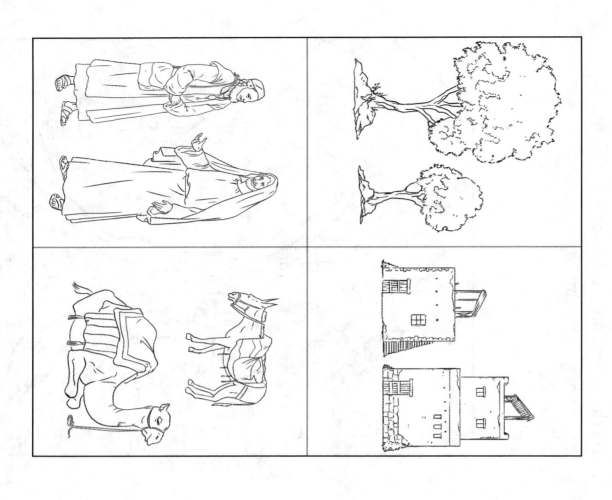

Connect the dots to see where Zacchaeus went so he could see Jesus.

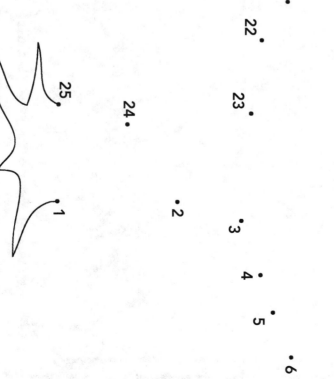

The Ten Talents

Luke 19:11-26

Jesus told a story about an angry and greedy king. He told this story because God's kingdom would be nothing like this man's kingdom.

Being greedy means not sharing and wanting everything for yourself. That's no fun! Draw something that you can share.

This story tells us what God is NOT like. Can you find ten words that describe what God is like?

```
L  H  O  P  E  A  C  E
N  J  O  Y  J  I  Y  X
G  L  Y  H  O  L  Y  Z
O  L  O  V  I  N  G  D
O  C  O  M  F  O  R  T
D  D  K  I  N  D  F  H
S  E  K  W  F  A  I  R
H  S  T  R  O  N  G  Y
```

HOLY   HOPE
GOOD   COMFORT
LOVING   JOY
KIND   FAIR
PEACE   STRONG

The king in the story was not very nice. Draw a picture of a grumpy king. Say a prayer of thanks that God isn't grumpy!

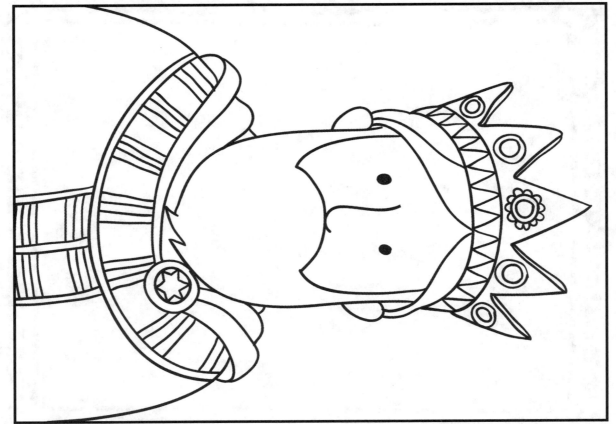

Jesus Enters Jerusalem

Luke 19:28-40

Jesus came into Jerusalem riding a donkey. The people were so excited to see him that they shouted out, "Blessings! Peace!"

The crowd waved palm branches as Jesus rode into town. Draw some palm trees.

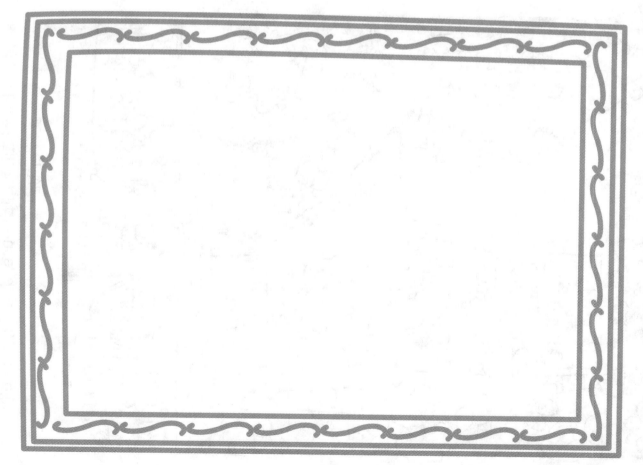

When Jesus entered the city, people yelled praises. Help Jesus find the way from Bethany to Jerusalem and find some other ways to praise God along the way.

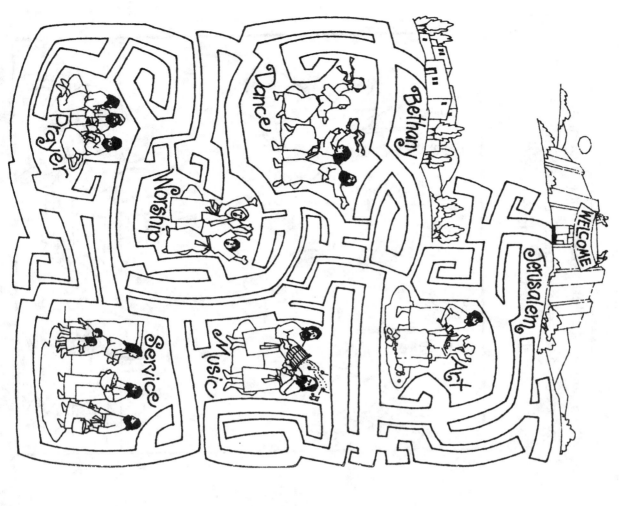

Find these items hidden in the picture: 3 palm branches, 3 cloaks/shirts, 2 animals, 2 sandals, an apple, a baseball, a birdhouse, a radio, a satellite dish, and a soccer ball.

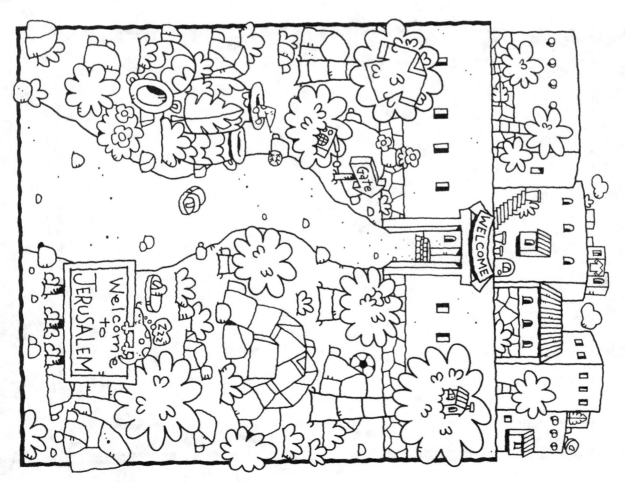

DEEP BLUE The Widow's Coins

Luke 21:1-4

Jesus saw a poor woman giving two copper coins in the temple. Two copper coins was a lot for her! It was all the money she had!

Draw a picture of something you can give to the church.

The woman had two coins to give. Cross out the coins below until there are only two coins left.

Circle the picture that is different from the others.

Jesus Celebrates Passover

Luke 22:7-20

Jesus had a special supper with his disciples. They shared bread and wine, and Jesus told them to have this meal over and over again to remember him.

Jesus celebrated Passover with his best friends. Draw a picture of you eating a meal with someone you love.

Jesus told each disciple to take a drink from his cup to remember that Jesus would always be with them. Connect the dots below to see the cup.

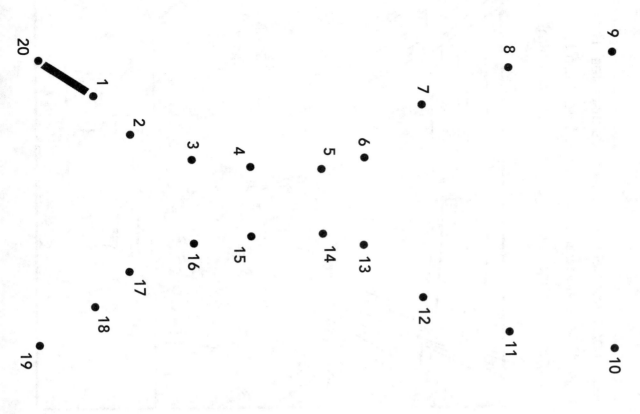

Jesus and the disciples ate in a room upstairs. Find the way through the maze to the upper room.

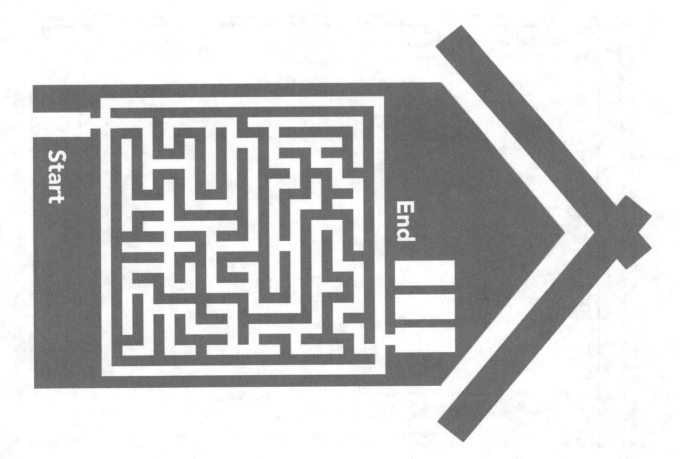

Start

End

The Tomb Is Empty
Luke 24:1-12

Mary Magdelene, Joanna, and Mary, James' mom, went to Jesus' tomb. When they arrived, the tomb was empty! Jesus's body wasn't there anymore! They ran to tell the disciples, "Jesus is alive!"

The women were the first people to share the good news that Jesus was alive again! Add yourself to the picture below – you can preach, too!

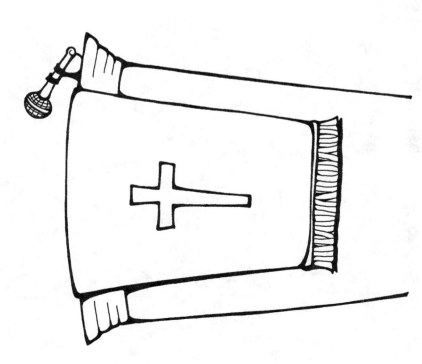

Connect the dots to see what Jesus' tomb might have looked like before Easter.

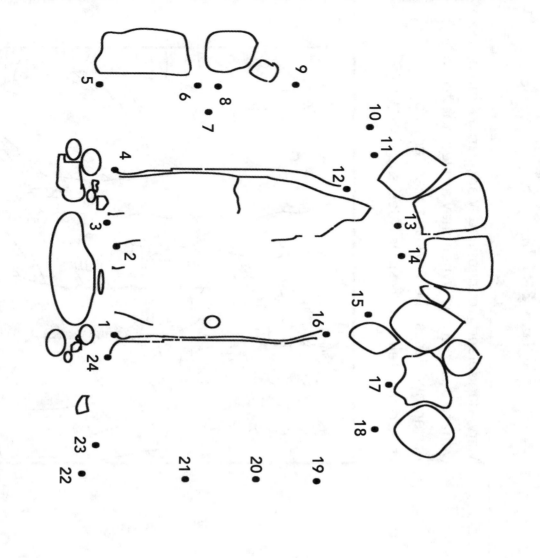

Jesus being alive again was a big surprise to the women. Draw a line to connect the picture of Mary Magdalene to the feeling in each picture.

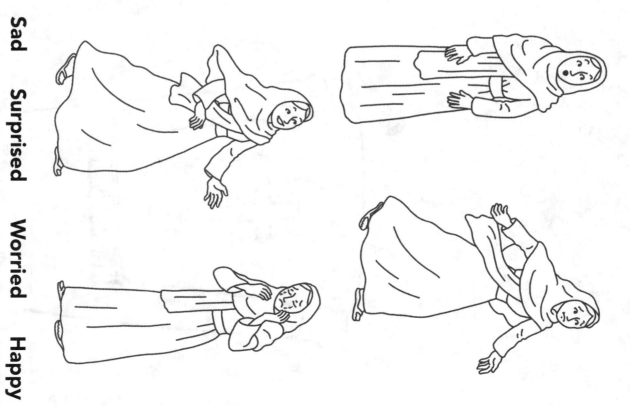

Sad   **Surprised**   **Worried**   **Happy**

The Road to Emmaus

Luke 24:13-35

Two friends were walking from Jerusalem to Emmaus. They were talking about how Jesus had died and was now alive again. Another man joined them. They didn't realize that the new person was Jesus!

Is there somewhere you like to walk with your friends? Draw yourself and your friends along the path.

Help the stranger and his two disciples get to Emmaus.

Who was walking with the friends?
Add that person to the picture.

Change the Water

John 2:1-12

Jesus was at a wedding when they ran out of wine to drink. Jesus took six big jars of water and turned the water into wine. It was a miracle!

Have you ever been to a wedding? Draw or describe it below.

Jesus turned the water into wine at a wedding.
Find the hidden objects in the picture.

Water and wine we kept in big jars. Draw lines
to connect the jars that look alike. Which jar is
different?

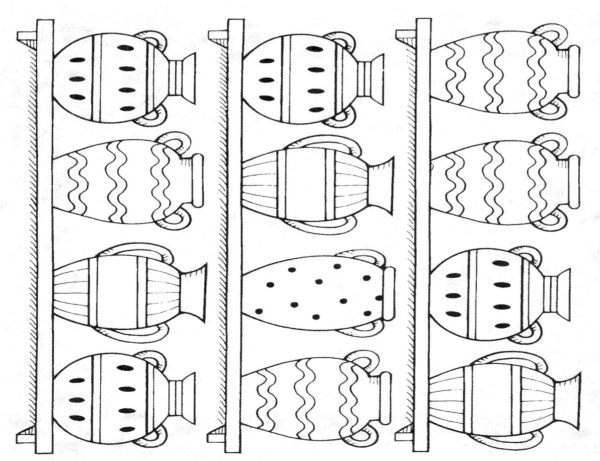

DEEP BLUE

Born Anew
John 3:1-21

Nicodemus was a religious man. He had questions for Jesus. Jesus answered, "God loved the world so much that God gave the world a special gift. That gift was God's Son."

God loves us so much! Fill this entire page with hearts!

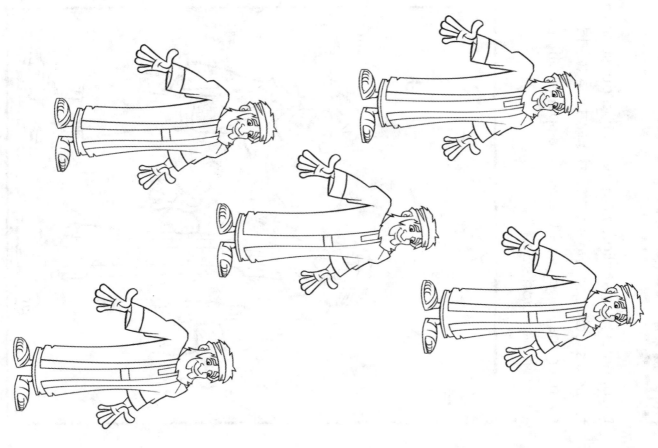

God gave the world a special gift - God's son, Jesus. Cross out every other letter to see why.

F	G	B	O	E
D	J	L	M	O
N	V	K	E	P
D	C	T	B	H
N	E	T	W	Q
O	Y	R	E	L
X	D	L	I	B

_ _ _ _ _ _ _ !

The Woman at the Well

John 4:1-42

A woman was getting water at the well. Jesus stopped to talk to her. She knew he must be God's Son because he already knew everything about her!

The woman went to the well to get water. Draw a picture of where you get water.

Help the woman find Jesus by the well.

The woman knew that Jesus was very special. Color the stones with a Z to reveal what she learned about him.

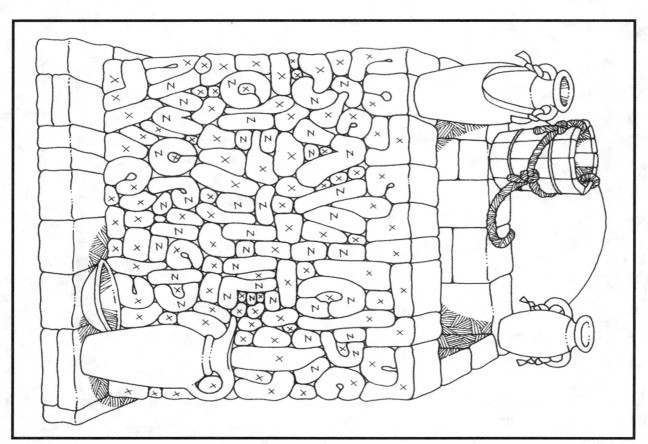

The Man by the Pool

John 5:1-17

Jesus healed a man who had not been able to walk for many years. He could walk again! Jesus knew the Jewish leaders would get angry, but Jesus helped people whenever he could, even on sabbath days.

Once Jesus healed him, the man could walk! Draw a map for him to follow.

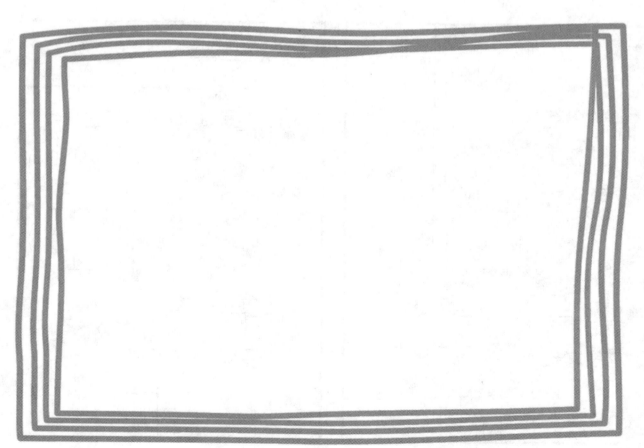

The Pharisees were mad at Jesus for healing the man on the sabbath day. Add their grumpy faces to the picture below.

Can you find eight differences between the two pictures?

A Boy's Lunch

John 6:1-15

Jesus used a boy's lunch of just five pieces of bread and two fish to feed a huge crowd of people. It was a miracle!

The boy packed fish and bread for lunch. What do you eat for lunch? Draw it below.

Circle the picture that shows how the disciples fed the crowd of people.

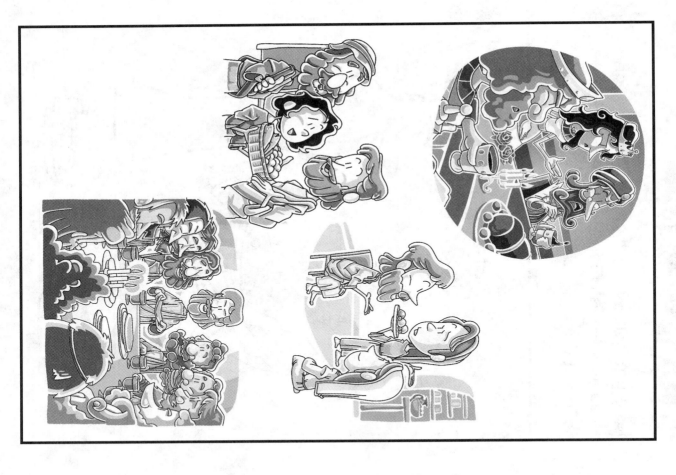

Which two pictures are exactly the same?

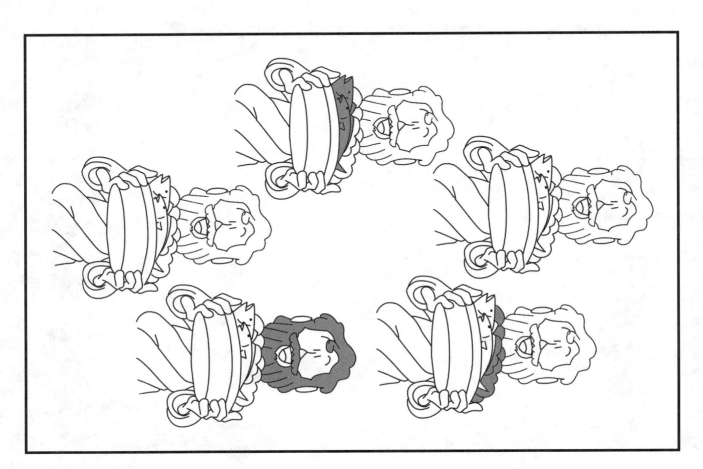

Jesus Walks on Water

John 6:16-25

Jesus went to pray on a mountain while the disciples took a boat to the other side of the lake. When Jesus was finished praying, he walked right on top of the water and into the boat!

Add Jesus to the picture. Where did he walk?

It was a stormy night. Add stars and the moon to the picture. Then cover up the stars with big, dark clouds to show the storm. How do you think the disciples felt?

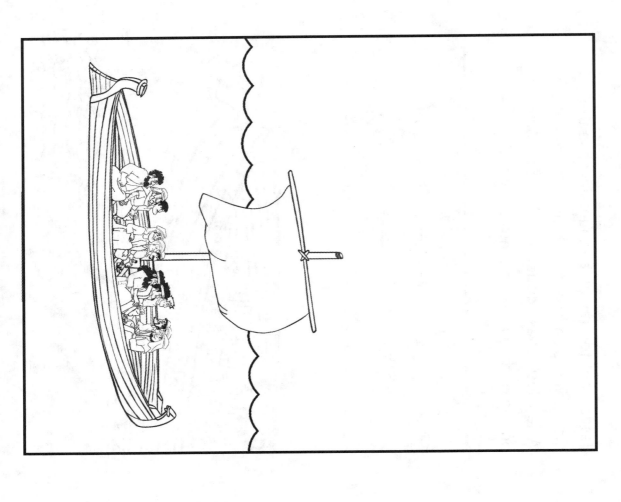

Peter walked on the water to Jesus and almost made it before he started to sink. Help Peter get to Jesus.

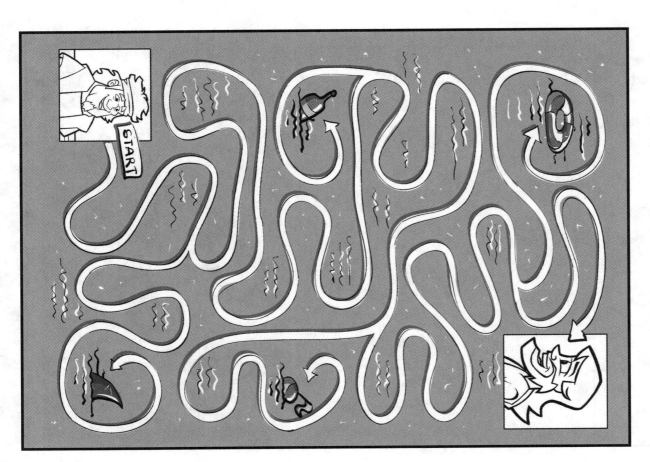

DEEP BLUE
Mary Honors Jesus
John 12:1-8

Mary gave Jesus a very special gift and was very kind to him. She loved him very much.

What's the most special gift you have given someone? Draw it in the frame below.

Mary rubbed Jesus' feet with perfume she had in a jar. Connect the dots to see what the jar looked like.

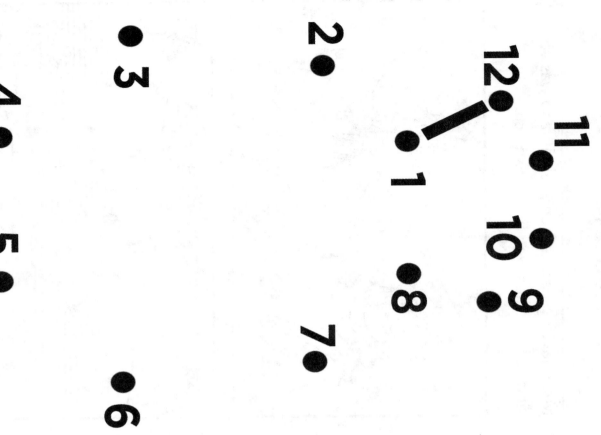

2
12
11
1
10
9
8
7
3
4
5
6

Mary gave Jesus a special present. How many presents can you find in the picture?

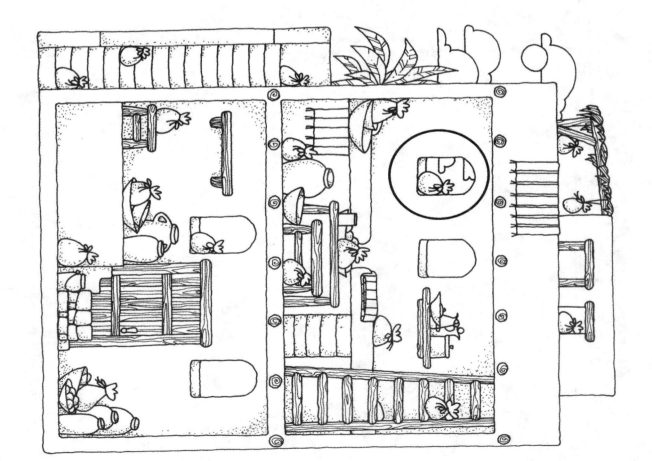

Jesus Washes Feet

John 13:1-17

Jesus washed the disciples' feet for them. He taught them that it is very important to serve one another.

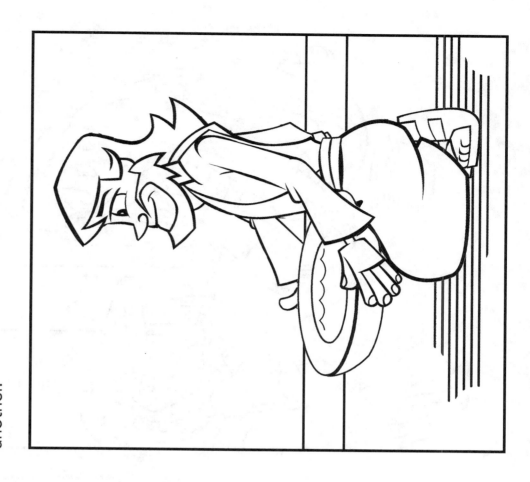

Jesus washed the disciples' feet before they ate. What do we usually wash before we eat?

What's missing? Complete the picture.

Jesus set an example for us to follow. He showed us how to be servants. Circle some of the ways you can be a servant, too.

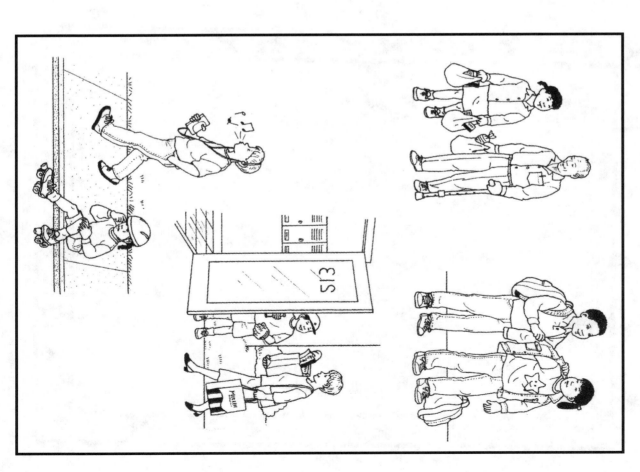

Jesus Lives

John 20:1-18

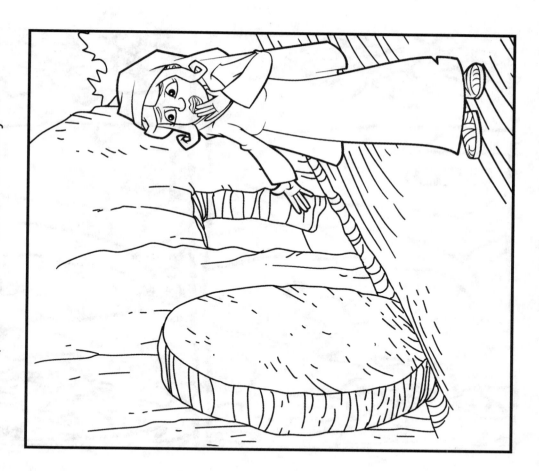

Mary Magdalene visited Jesus' tomb where his body was buried. His body wasn't there anymore! Then a man talked to her – it was Jesus! He told her, "Mary, tell the disciples that I am alive." So Mary did!

Mary told the disciples the good news that Jesus was alive. Who can you tell? Draw them in the frame below.

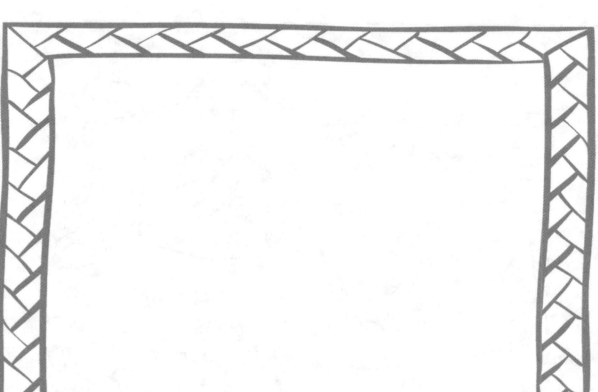

When Mary went to the tomb, it was empty!
Find 6 differences between the pictures.

Circle the picture where Mary feels glad. Draw an X through the pictures where Mary is sad. What made her so happy?

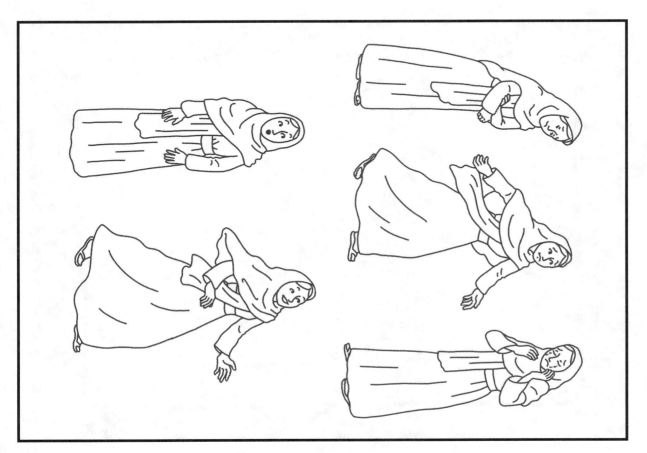

DEEP BLUE Thomas Believes
John 20:24-31

Jesus, who had died but was alive again, visited the disciples. Thomas wasn't with them, so he didn't get to see Jesus. Jesus visited them again so that Thomas could see him alive again!

Draw a picture of something you believe in even though you haven't seen it.

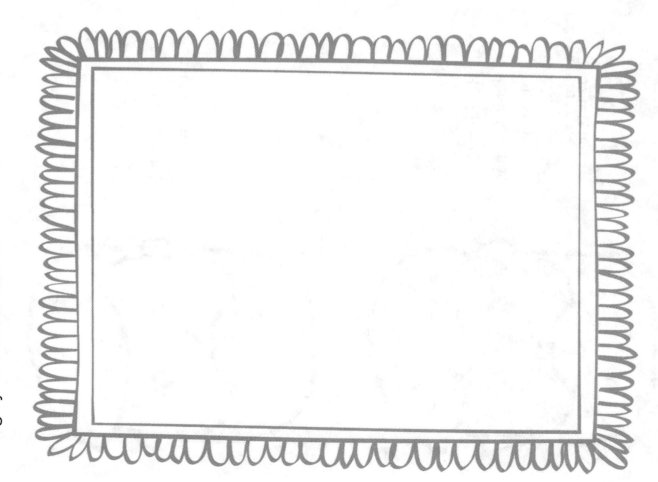

Write the first letter of each animal in the blank to see which disciple was missing when Jesus visited them.

___ ___ ___ ___ ___ ___

Thomas was sad that he didn't get to see Jesus.

Give Thomas a sad face.

How do you think Thomas felt after Jesus visited him?

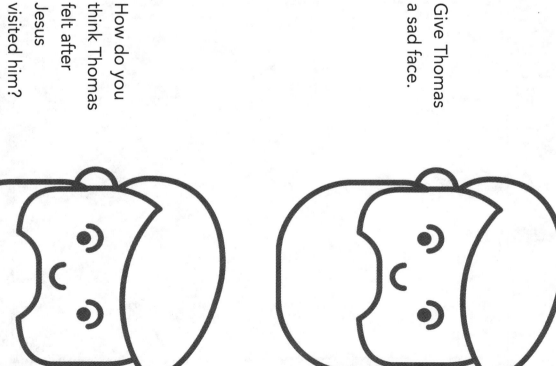

Come to Breakfast!

John 21:1-14

The disciples were fishing early in the morning when Jesus, who had died but was alive again, visited them. They had breakfast together on the beach.

What did you eat for breakfast today? Draw it in the frame below.

Fishermen used nets to catch fish.
Connect the dots to see one.

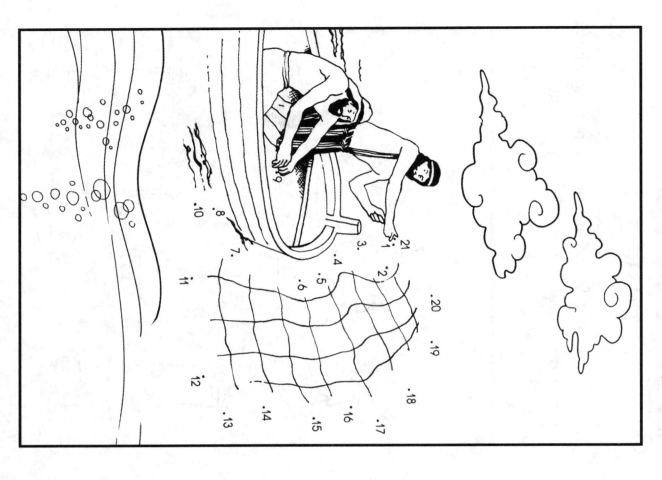

Jesus and the disciples ate fish on the beach.
Can you find seven fish hidden in the picture?

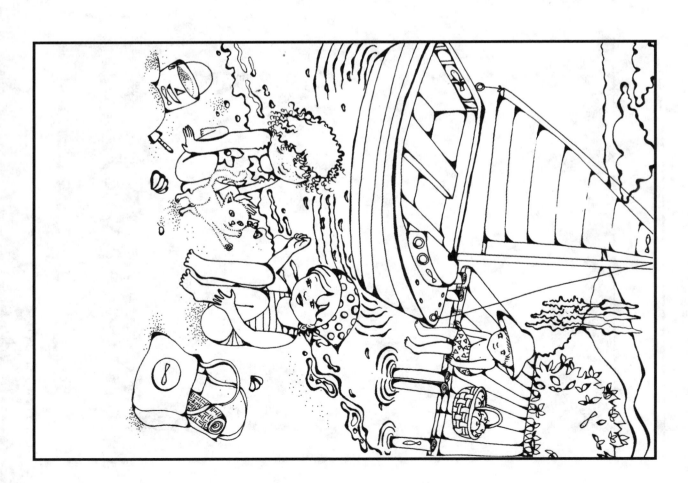

Feed My Sheep

John 21:15-19

Jesus, who had died but was alive again, was eating breakfast with the disciples. He asked Peter, "Peter, do you love me?" Peter said, "Yes, Jesus, you know that I love you." Jesus told Peter to share God's love with everyone.

Do you have a brother, sister, friend, or pet you take care of? Draw them in the frame below.

We are Jesus' sheep. Jesus takes good care of us like a good shepherd. Help the shepherd find the hidden sheep in the picture below.

Jesus told Peter to take care of people the way a good shepherd takes care of sheep. Connect the dots to see what a loving shepherd might do.

Pentecost

Acts 2:1-41

God gave the disciples the Holy Spirit, which helped them speak and preach in special ways. Lots of people decided to follow Jesus when they heard the disciples!

What do you think the Holy Spirit looks like?

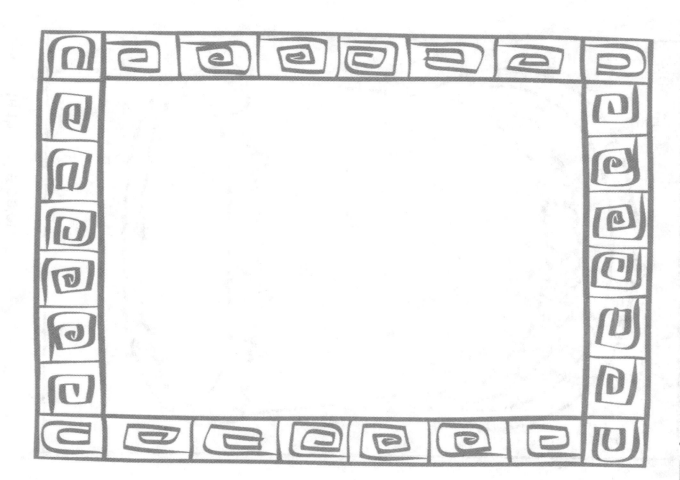

The dove is a symbol of the Holy Spirit.
Connect the dots in alphabetical order.

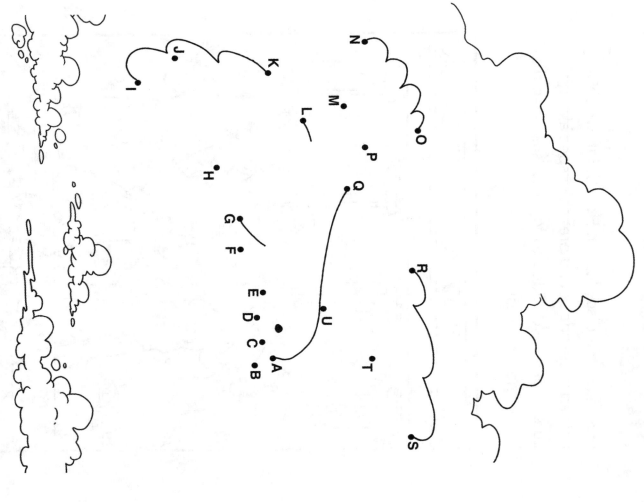

Pentecost is the church's birthday.
Decorate the cake below.

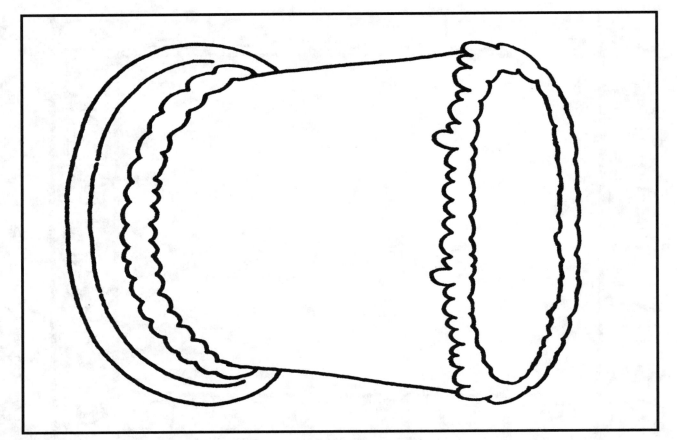

Peter and John

Acts 3:1–4:22

John and Peter saw a man who couldn't walk. The man's friends had to carry him everywhere. Peter healed the man. It was a miracle!

The man depended on his friends. Draw a picture of someone you can depend on to give you help when you need it.

People gave the man money to help him live.
Color the gifts the people gave him.

Help Peter and John find their way to the man they
will heal.

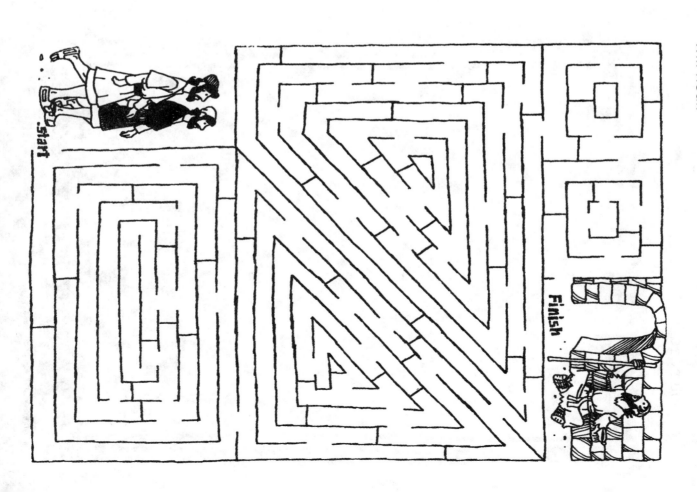

Start

Finish

DEEP BLUE

Believers Share

Acts 4:32-37

The people who believed in Jesus shared their food and belongings. Everybody had what they needed because everybody shared!

Draw something you can share with a friend or family member.

The believers divided up their food so everybody had enough. Can you get each fruit to the right box?

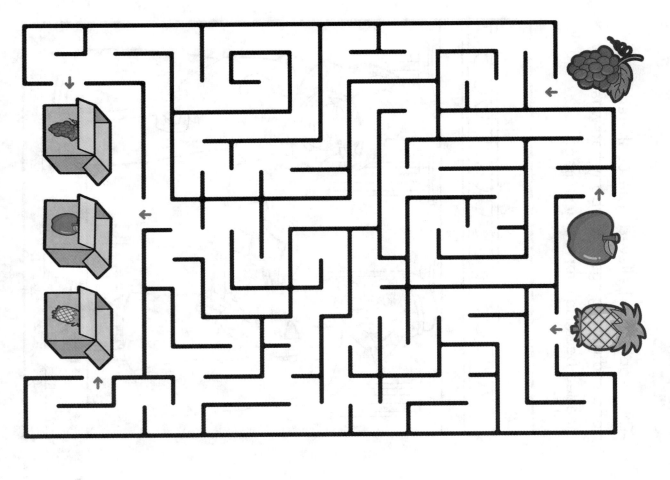

Put a check mark by the people who are sharing. Put an X by the people who are not.

DEEP BLUE

Choosing the Seven

Acts 6:1-7

So many people were choosing to believe in Jesus that the disciples couldn't take care of everybody by themselves. They chose seven people to help them.

What is something you love? Draw it 7 times.

Help get the food to the widows and orphans. Start from the food and find the paths to each of the groups of people.

The disciples chose leaders to serve their community. Circle the ways you can serve this week. Pick one way and do it!

Philip and the Ethiopian

Acts 8:26-40

Philip saw a man reading a scroll and asked if he could help the man, who was from a faraway land. The scroll was all about Jesus. Philip taught the man about Jesus and baptized him. He had decided to follow Jesus!

If you made up a language, what would it look like? Draw a sample of it in the frame. What does it say?

Follow the road to help Philip get to the Ethiopian man in the chariot.

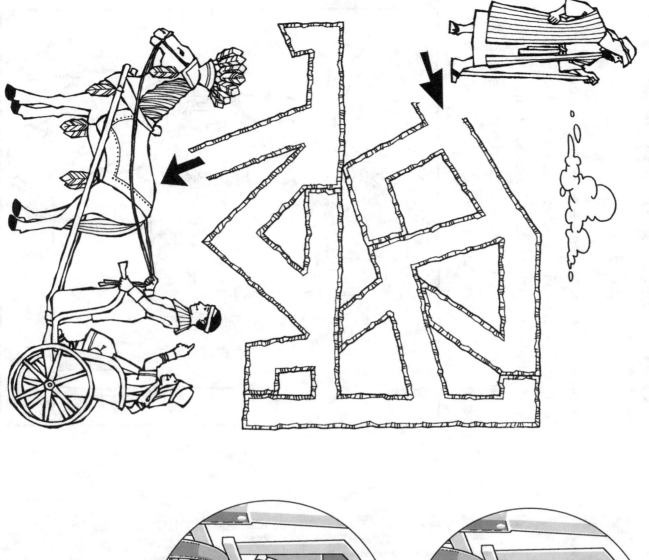

Can you find the two pictures that are the same?

Paul Changes
Acts 9:1-19

Paul's job was to arrest people who believed in Jesus. Paul didn't like Jesus or his followers. Then God spoke to him and told him to help the believers instead. Paul became a follower of Jesus. What a big change!

We change a lot growing up. Draw a picture of yourself as a baby. How have you changed since then?

Ananias was a Christian who helped Paul.
Can you show Ananias the way to Paul?

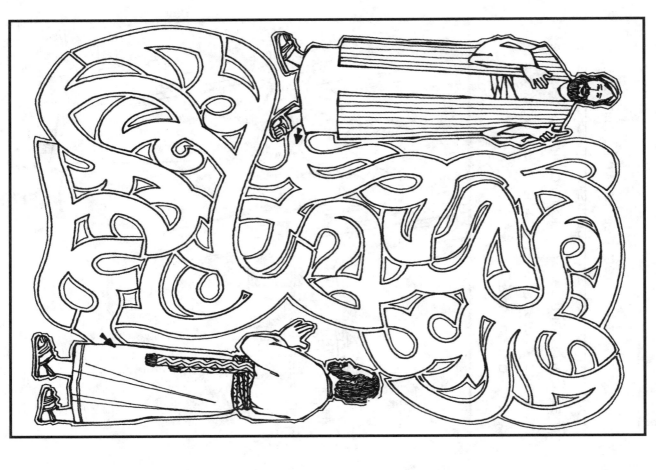

Changes on the outside are easy to see. Changes on the inside, like Paul's big change, are not. Put an X on any changes you see between the first and second pictures.

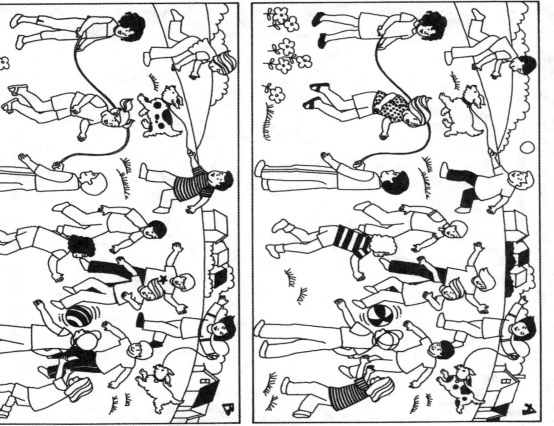

DEEP BLUE Paul Escapes
Acts 9:20-25

Paul wanted to tell everyone about Jesus, but some people did not believe he had really changed. Some of these people got so mad at Paul that they wanted to hurt him. Paul's friends helped him sneak out of the city in a basket.

Draw a safe place for Paul to escape.

Connect the dots to see how Paul's friends helped him escape.

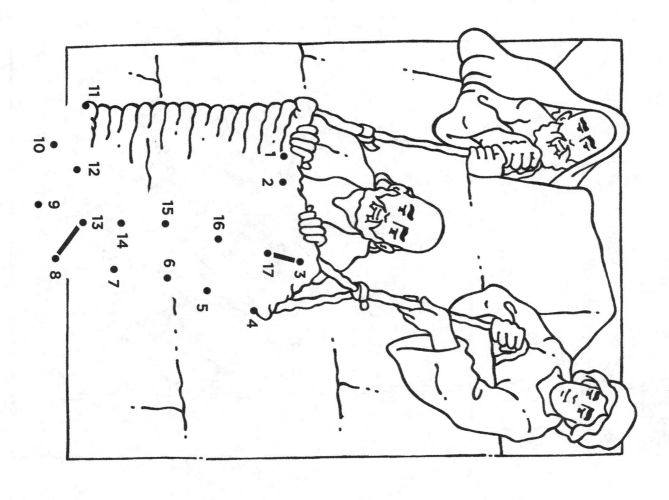

Help Paul escape from Damascus.

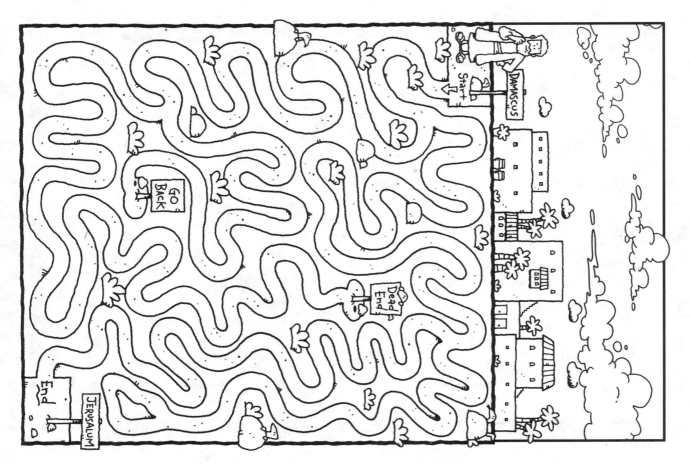

At first, the disciples weren't sure if Paul had changed. Their friend Barnabas told them Paul's story. The disciples trusted Barnabas, so they believed him and let Paul help. The church grew and grew!

Lots and lots of people decided to follow Jesus' teaching. Fill the frame with as many people as you can.

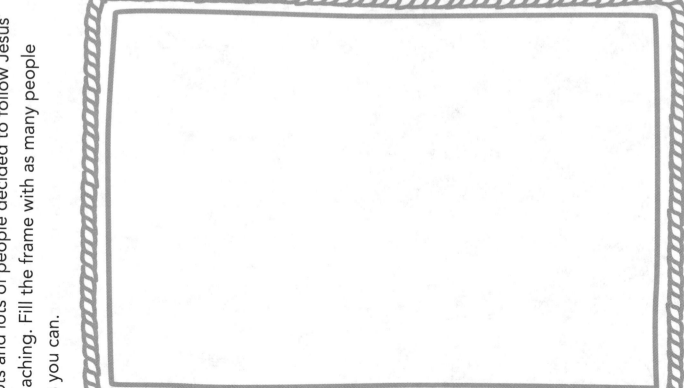

As Paul and Barnabas taught, more and more people believed.

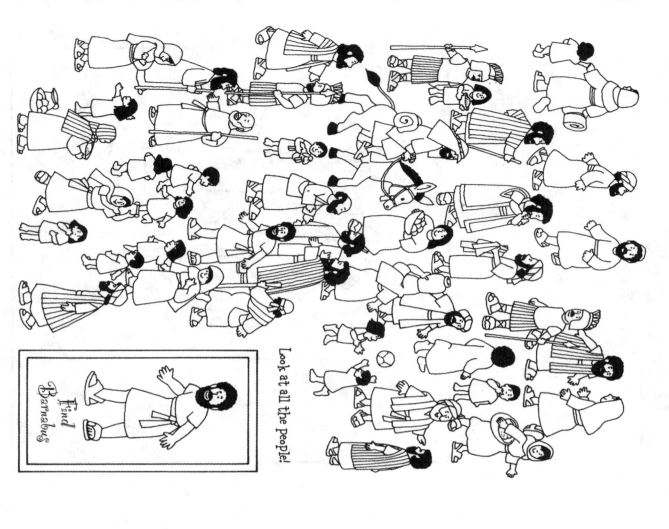

Look at all the people!

Find Barnabas

Barnabas taught the believers to treat each other with love. Circle the pictures below that show what the believers did. Draw an X on the pictures showing what the disciples didn't do.

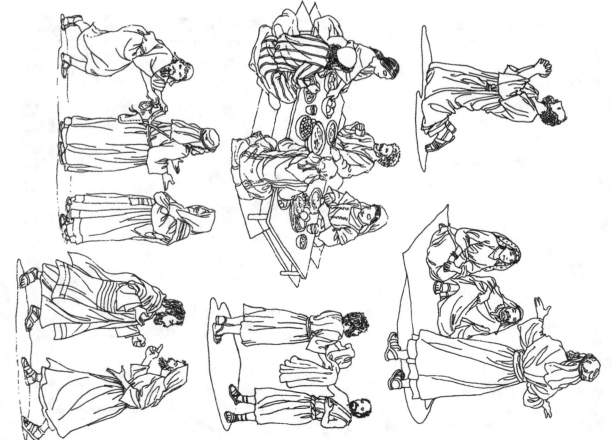

Peter and Tabitha

Acts 9:36-43

A disciple named Tabitha was very kind. She got sick and died. Everyone was sad! Peter prayed for her and God made her alive again. It was a miracle!

Turn this sad face into a happy face!

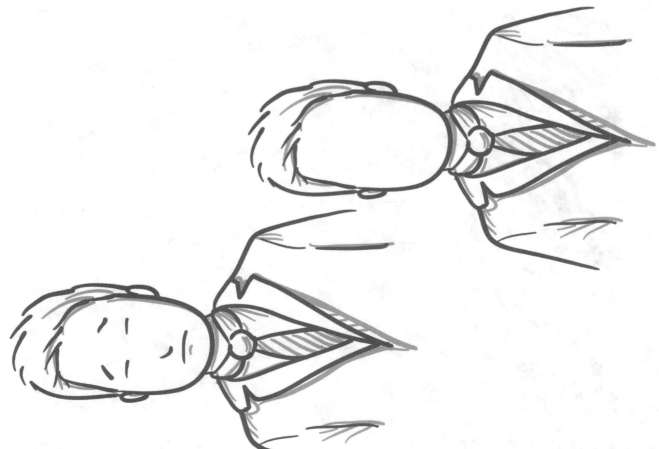

Caterpillars in cocoons don't look very alive – but God turns them into butterflies! God gave Tabitha new life, too. Draw the blank halves to look like the completed halves.

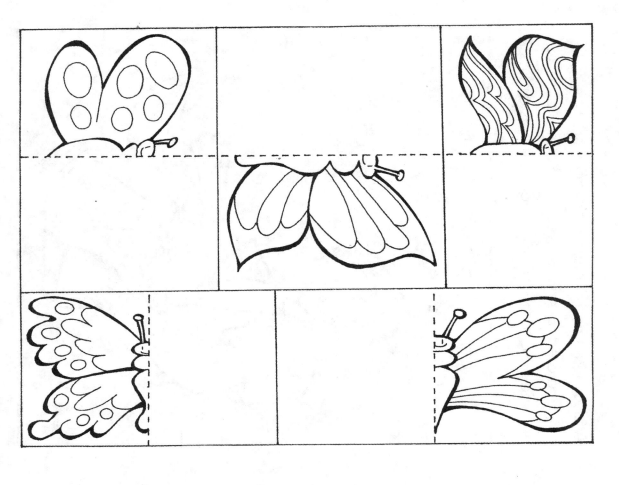

Circle the things that shouldn't be in this picture.

Peter and Cornelius

Acts 10:1-28

Peter thought believers should only eat certain kinds of foods. Cornelius disagreed. Cornelius helped Peter understand that every person and every animal that God makes is good.

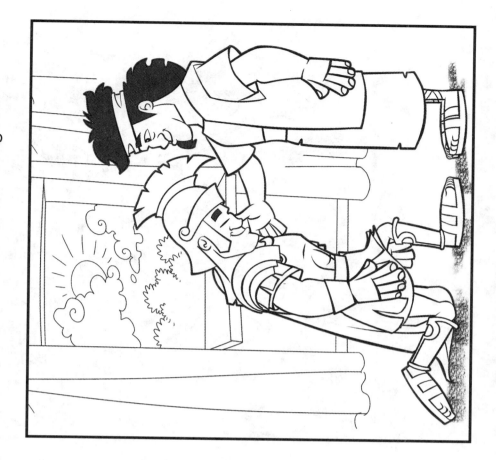

Draw foods from three different food groups.

Find the differences between the two pictures.

At first, there were some foods the believers were not allowed to eat. They could eat quail, cow, goat, chicken, and fish. After this story, the believers could eat any food. Circle the food they could eat before and color the food they could eat after.

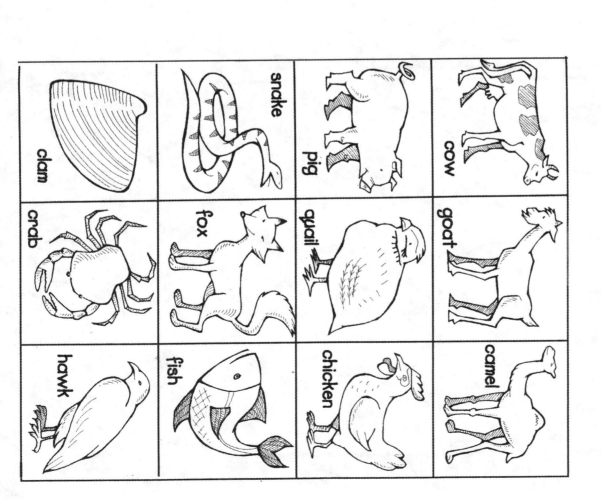

cow	goat	camel
pig	quail	chicken
snake	fox	fish
clam	crab	hawk

First Called Christians

Acts 11:19-30

Barnabas went to a town called Antioch to teach people about Jesus. Paul joined him later to help. The people of Antioch called the believers "Christians."

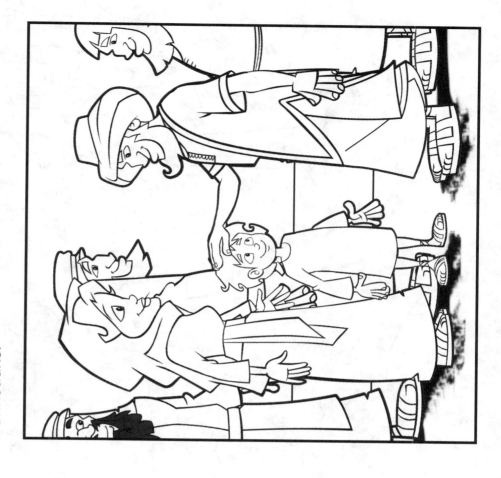

Do you or anyone in your family have a nickname? Draw the person and write their nickname in the frame below.

The early Christians used a picture of a fish to tell who was a Christian. They would draw it in the sand, and if the other person was a Christian, they would finish the drawing. The fish symbol looks like this: ⟩. Can you finish it in the picture below?

Help Barnabas and Saul find their way from Antioch to Judea to share with Christians there.

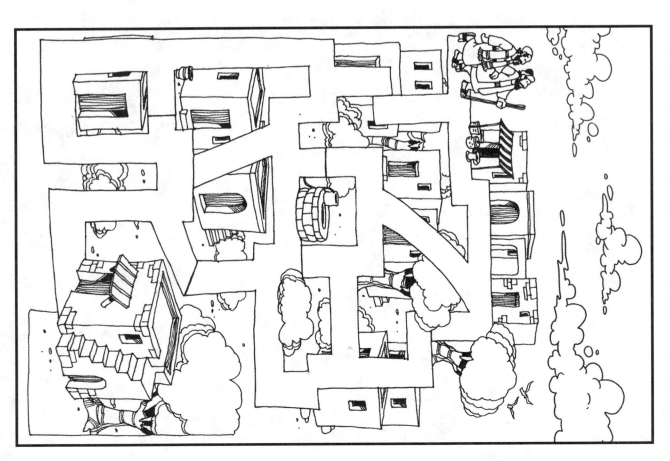

Peter in Prison

DEEP BLUE

Acts 12:1-17

King Herod put Peter in jail for telling people about Jesus. An angel set Peter free. Peter went to Mary's house, where she and her friends had been praying for him. They were very excited that he was out of jail!

Draw Peter in jail. Then draw Peter running free!

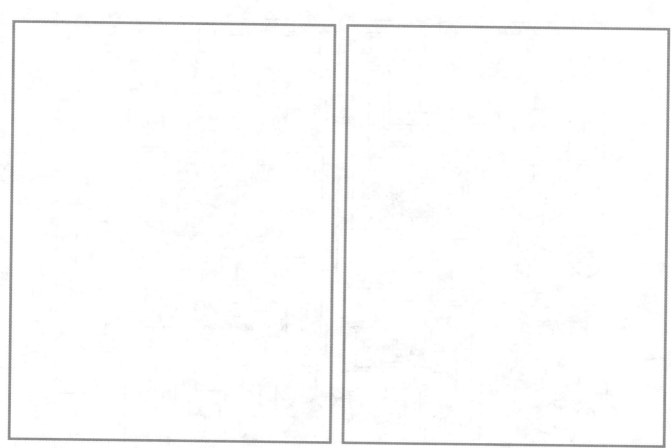

When the angel appeared to Peter, the chains Peter was locked up in fell off.

How many locks do you count below? ____

How many of the locks are open? ____

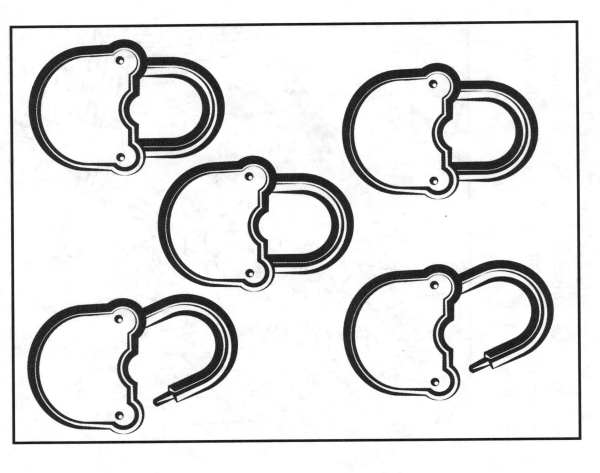

Lead Peter to the church. Make sure you pass all the angels and avoid all of the guards.

Timothy Is Chosen

Acts 16:1-5

Paul loved Jesus and spent a lot of time teaching others about Jesus. A boy named Timothy helped him.

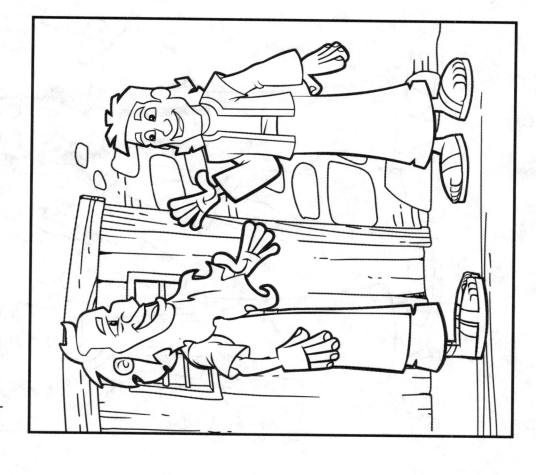

Timothy helped Paul. Draw a picture of yourself helping your pastor. You can be in ministry, too!

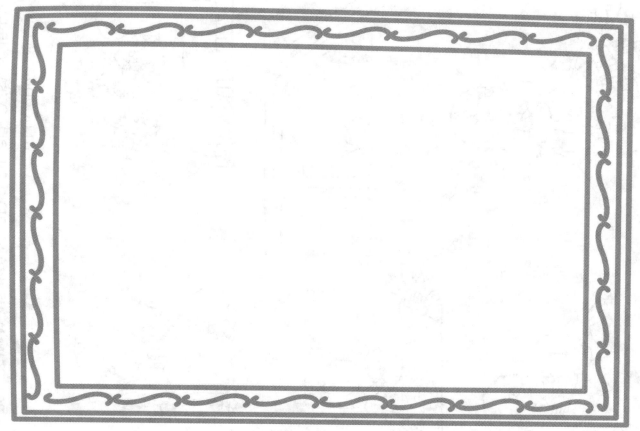

Can you find 7 differences between the two pictures of Timothy?

As a kid, there are some things that you aren't big enough to do. But you are big enough to help in other ways! Circle the pictures that show what you are big enough to do.

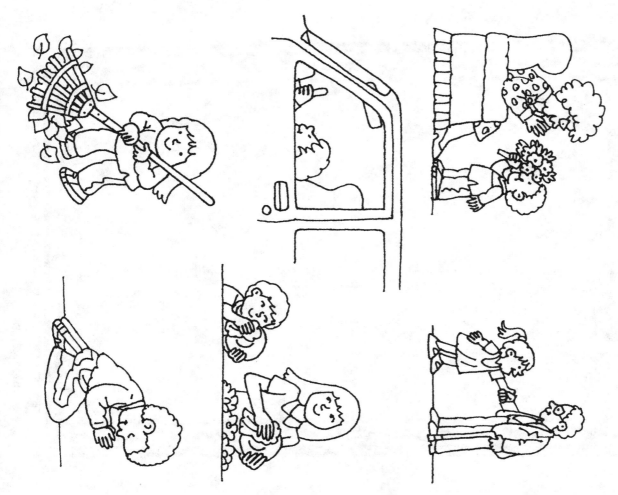

DEEP BLUE

Lydia

Acts 16:11-15

Lydia was a powerful woman who believed in God. Paul told her about Jesus. She and her family decided to follow Jesus and were baptized. Lydia helped Paul tell others about Jesus.

Lydia sold purple cloth. If you had a store, what would you sell? Draw the items below.

Help Paul find his way to Lydia.

What did Lydia do when she decided to follow Jesus? Fill in the letters to see.

★ = S   ▲ = A   〰 = E

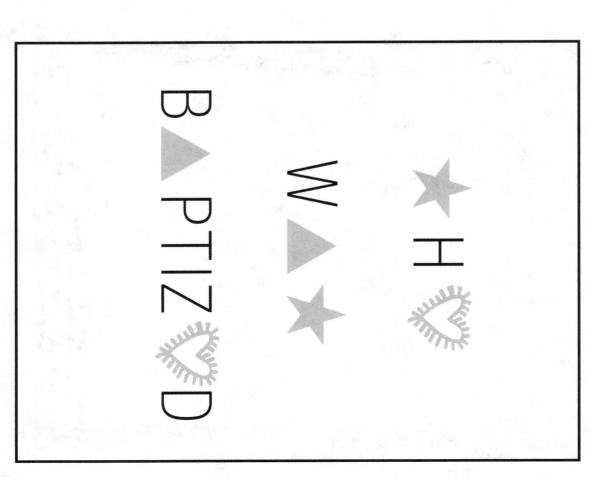

B▲PTIZ〰D

★H〰

W▲★

 **Paul and Silas**
Acts 16:16-40

Paul and Silas were in jail because some people didn't want them to tell people about Jesus. An earthquake broke the jail open, and they were free. But Paul and Silas stayed with the jailer so that that he didn't get in trouble.

Paul and Silas told the jailer about Jesus. Who can you tell about Jesus? Draw them in the frame below.

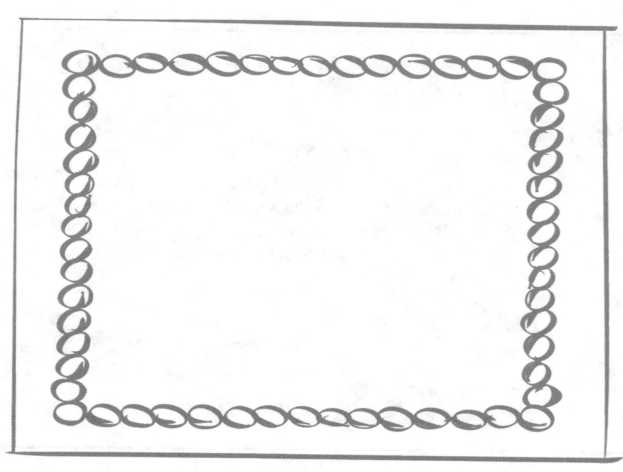

143

Paul and Silas were locked in the jail. Can you find 10 keys in the picture below?

Paul and Silas were good ministry partners. You can be a good partner, too. Draw lines to connect the partners below.

Shipwrecked

Acts 27:1-44

Paul was on a boat that sailed into a huge storm. The boat almost sank! God helped everyone on the boat get to an island. They were safe! Draw a storm and angry ocean waves.

Draw a picture of the island where the ship wrecked.

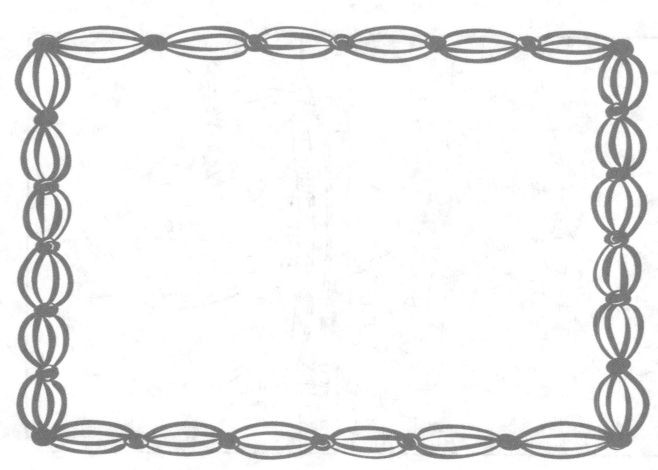

Paul told the people on the ship to eat so they would be strong for what? Cross out the letters **P-A-U-L** to see. Write the remaining letters on the line.

line. _____

P	S	W	U	I
M	M	A	I	P
N	U	G	T	A
O	A	S	L	H
L	O	P	R	E

Connect the dots to see what the ship might have looked like.

DEEP BLUE
We Are One Body
1 Corinthians 12:12-31

Paul taught the believers in Corinth that everybody has a special gift. No one person is any more important than any other. The church needs everyone's gifts.

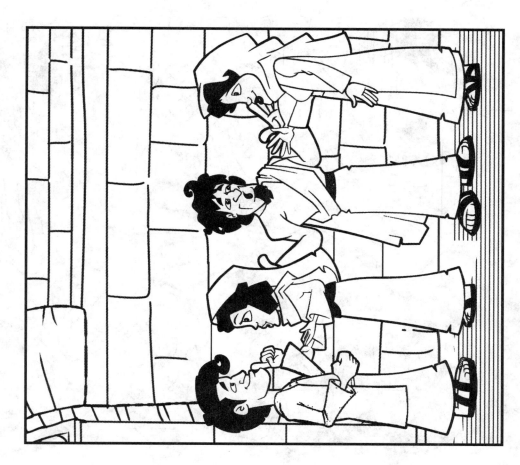

Each person is important. You have special gifts and talents that are a part of who you are. Draw a picture of yourself doing something that you like to do.

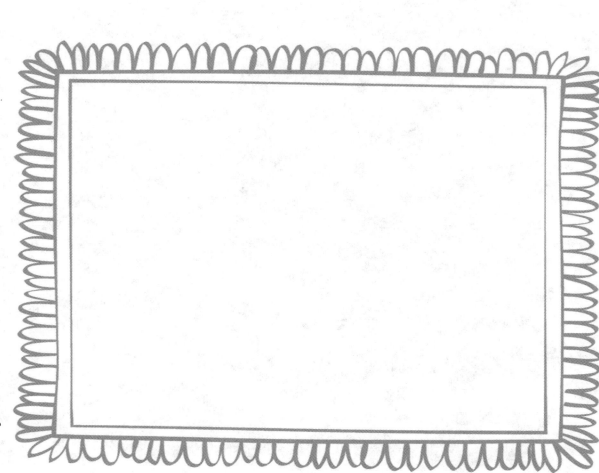

Paul wrote letters to the Christians in many cities.
Starting from the center of the maze, help get
Paul's letters to the churches in the different cities.

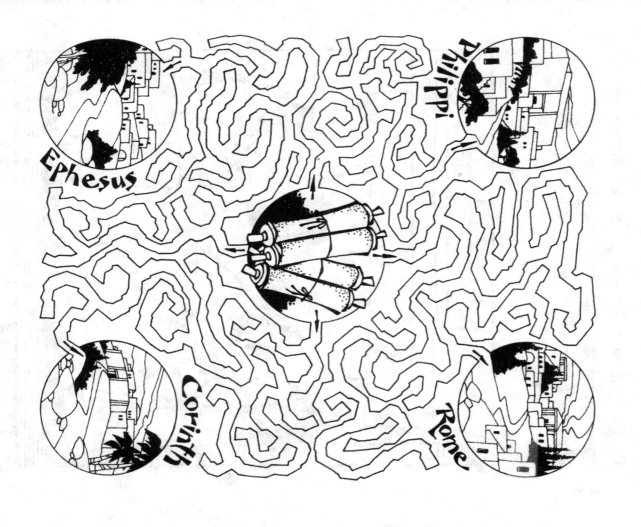

Ephesus

Philippi

Corinth

Rome

Just like every part of our bodies is important,
every person in the church is important. Connect
the dots. Then label hands, head, ears, and knees.

Love

1 Corinthians 13:1-13

Paul taught the believers in Corinth about love.
He wrote them a letter that said, "Love is patient.
Love is kind. Love isn't jealous. Love doesn't brag.
Love isn't rude."

Love is kind. Draw a beautiful picture and give it to someone you love.

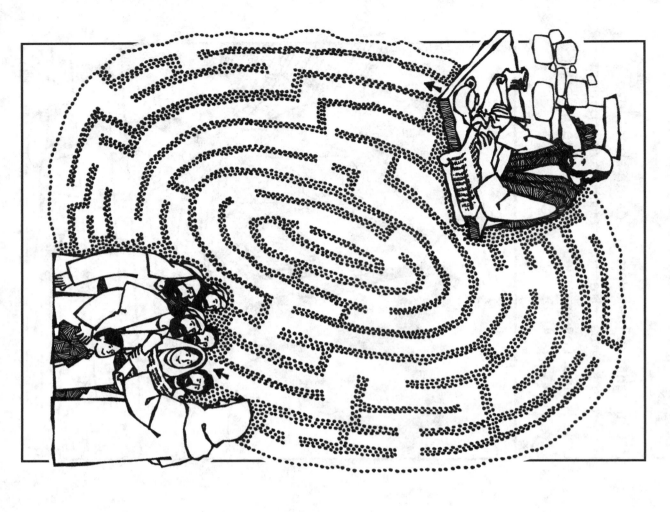

Who should we love? Fill in the blanks to see!

♥ = O   ☺ = E

L V ♥ G D   A C H
— — — —   — — —
L ♥ ☺ ♥   ♥ ♥
AND
L V G D   T H R
— — — —   — — —
♥ ☺ ♥   ♥ ☺

Lectionary Index

Year A

Lectionary Date	Story	Bulletin Number
1st Sunday of Advent	N/A	
2nd Sunday of Advent	The Peaceable Kingdom (Isaiah 11:6-9)	56
3rd Sunday of Advent	Mary Visits Elizabeth (Luke 1:38-66)	89
4th Sunday of Advent	Joseph's Story (Matthew 1:18-24)	62
Christmas Eve	Jesus is Born (Luke 2:1-7)	90
	Joyous News (Luke 2:8-20)	91
1st Sunday after Christmas Day	N/A	
Epiphany of the Lord	Follow the Star (Matthew 2:1-12)	63
Baptism of the Lord	Come to the River (Matthew 3:13-17)	64
2nd Sunday after Epiphany	N/A	
3rd Sunday after Epiphany	Jesus Calls the Fishermen (Matthew 4:18-22)	65
4th Sunday after Epiphany	Peace (Matthew 5:1-9)	66
5th Sunday after Epiphany	N/A	
6th Sunday after Epiphany	N/A	
7th Sunday after Epiphany	N/A	
8th Sunday after Epiphany	The Birds of the Air (Matthew 6:25-34)	68
Transfiguration Sunday	N/A	
Ash Wednesday	The Lord's Prayer (Matthew 6:5-15)	67
1st Sunday in Lent	Adam and Eve (Genesis 2:10-3:24)	4
2nd Sunday in Lent	Abraham and Sarah (Genesis 12:1-9, 15:1-6)	9
	Born Anew (John 3:1-21)	118
3rd Sunday in Lent	The Woman at the Well (John 4:1-42)	119
4th Sunday in Lent	Samuel Anoints David (1 Samuel 16:1-23)	37
	Gentleness (Psalm 23:1-6)	53
5th Sunday in Lent	N/A	
Passion/Palm Sunday	Hosanna! (Matthew 21:1-11)	73
	At the Last Supper (Matthew 26:17-30)	74
	In the Garden (Matthew 26:31-58)	75
	Cock-a-doodle-doo! (Matthew 26:69-75)	76
Holy/Maundy Thursday	Jesus Washes Feet (John 13:1-17)	124
Good Friday	N/A	
Easter Day	Jesus Lives! (John 20:1-18)	125
	Alleluia! (Matthew 28:1-10)	77
2nd Sunday of Easter	Thomas Believes (John 20:24-31)	126
	Pentecost (Acts 2:1-21)	129
3rd Sunday of Easter	The Road to Emmaus (Luke 24:13-35)	116
	Pentecost (Acts 2:1-21)	129
4th Sunday of Easter	Believers Share (Acts 4:32-37)	131
	Gentleness (Psalm 23:1-6)	53
5th Sunday of Easter	N/A	

Lectionary Date (Year A)	Story	Bulletin Number
6th Sunday of Easter	N/A	
Ascension	N/A	
7th Sunday of Easter	N/A	
Day of Pentecost	Pentecost (Acts 2:1-21)	129
Trinity Sunday (1st Sunday after Pentecost)	The Earth (Genesis 1:1-19)	1
	Living Things (Genesis 1:20-25)	2
	In God's Image (Genesis 1:26-2:4)	3
	The Great Commission (Matthew 28:16-20)	78
May 29—June 4 inclusive (if after Trinity)	Noah Builds the Ark (Genesis 6:13-22)	5
	Sending Out the Dove (Genesis 8:1-19)	7
	The Two Houses (Matthew 7:24-27)	70
June 5—June 11 inclusive (if after Trinity)	Abraham and Sarah (Genesis 12:1-9, 15:1-6)	9
June 12—June 18 inclusive (if after Trinity)	The Birth of Isaac (Genesis 18:1-15, 21:1-7)	11
June 19—June 25 inclusive (if after Trinity)	N/A	
June 26—July 2 inclusive	N/A	
July 3—July 9 inclusive	Isaac and Rebecca (Genesis 24:1-67)	12
July 10—July 16 inclusive	Jacob and Esau (Genesis 25:19-28)	13
	The Birthright (Genesis 25:29-34)	14
July 17—July 23 inclusive	Jacob's Ladder (Genesis 28: 10-22)	16
July 24—July 30 inclusive	N/A	
July 31—August 6 inclusive	N/A	
August 7—August 13 inclusive	Joseph and His Brothers (Genesis 37:1-36)	17
August 14—August 20 inclusive	Joseph and His Brothers Reunited (Genesis 42:1–46:34	20
August 21—August 27 inclusive	The Baby in the Basket (Exodus 1:8-14, 2:1-10)	21
August 28—September 3 inclusive	The Burning Bush (Exodus 2:11–3:22)	22
September 4—September 10 inclusive	Moses and Pharaoh (Exodus 5:1–13:9)	23
September 11—September 17 inclusive	Crossing the Sea (Exodus 13:17–14:31)	24
	Songs of Joy (Exodus 15:1-21)	25
September 18—September 24 inclusive	In the Wilderness (Exodus 15:22–17:7)	26
September 25—October 1 inclusive	In the Wilderness (Exodus 15:22–17:7)	26
October 2—October 8 inclusive	Ten Commandments (Exodus 19:1–20:21)	27
October 9—October 15 inclusive	N/A	
October 16—October 22 inclusive	N/A	
October 23—October 29 inclusive	N/A	
October 30—November 5 inclusive	Crossing the Jordan (Joshua 3:7-17)	31
All Saints Day	Peace (Matthew 5:1-9)	66
November 6—November 12 inclusive	N/A	
November 13—November 19 inclusive	N/A	
Christ the King	Joy (Psalm 100:1-5)	54
Thanksgiving Day	Ten Lepers (Luke 17:11-19)	107

Year B

Lectionary Date	Story	Bulletin Number
1st Sunday of Advent	N/A	
2nd Sunday of Advent	N/A	
3rd Sunday of Advent	N/A	
4th Sunday of Advent	Gabriel's Message (Luke 1:26-38)	88
	Mary Visits Elizabeth (Luke1:39-66)	89
Christmas Eve	Jesus is Born (Luke 2:1-7)	90
	Joyous News (Luke 2:8-20)	91
1st Sunday after Christmas Day	Simeon and Anna (Luke 2:25-31)	92
Epiphany of the Lord	Follow the Star (Matthew 2:1-12)	63
Baptism of the Lord	The Earth (Genesis 1:1-19)	1
	A Voice in the Wilderness (Mark 1:9-11)	79
2nd Sunday after Epiphany	God Calls Samuel (1 Samuel 3:1-21)	35
3rd Sunday after Epiphany	Jonah and the Fish (Jonah 1–4)	61
4th Sunday after Epiphany	N/A	
5th Sunday after Epiphany	N/A	
6th Sunday after Epiphany	Elisha and the Servant Girl (2 Kings 5:1-19)	51
7th Sunday after Epiphany	The Four Friends (Mark 2:1-12)	80
8th Sunday after Epiphany	N/A	
Transfiguration Sunday	N/A	
Ash Wednesday	The Lord's Prayer (Matthew 6:5-15)	67
1st Sunday in Lent	The Rainbow Promise (Genesis 8:20–9:17)	8
	A Voice in the Wilderness (Mark 1:9-11)	79
2nd Sunday in Lent	N/A	
3rd Sunday in Lent	Ten Commandments (Exodus 19:1–20:21)	27
4th Sunday in Lent	Born Anew (John 3:1-21)	118
5th Sunday in Lent	N/A	
Passion/Palm Sunday	People Welcome Jesus (Mark 11:1-11)	85
	Jesus Breaks the Bread (Mark 14:12-26)	86
Holy/Maundy Thursday	Moses and Pharaoh (Exodus 5:1–13:9)	23
	Jesus Washes Feet (John 13:1-17)	124
Good Friday	N/A	
Easter Day	Jesus Lives! (John 20:1-18)	125
2nd Sunday of Easter	Thomas Believes (John 20:24-31)	126
	Believers Share (Acts 4:32-37)	131
3rd Sunday of Easter	Peter and John (Acts 3:1–4:22)	130
4th Sunday of Easter	Peter and John (Acts 3:1–4:22)	130
	Gentleness (Psalm 23:1-6)	53
5th Sunday of Easter	Philip and the Ethiopian (Acts 8:26-40)	133
6th Sunday of Easter	N/A	
Ascension	N/A	
7th Sunday of Easter	N/A	
Day of Pentecost	Pentecost (Acts 2:1-21)	129

Lectionary Date (Year B)	Story	Bulletin Number
Trinity Sunday (1st Sunday after Pentecost)	Born Anew (John 3:1-21)	118
May 29—June 4 inclusive (if after Trinity)	N/A	
June 5—June 11 inclusive (if after Trinity)	Samuel Annoints Saul (1 Samuel 7:15–8:22; 10:17-24)	36
June 12—June 18 inclusive (if after Trinity)	Samuel Annoints David (1 Samuel 16:1-23)	37
June 19—June 25 inclusive (if after Trinity)	David and Goliath (1 Samuel 17:1-51)	39
	Jesus Calms the Storm (Mark 4:35-42)	81
June 26—July 2 inclusive	Jairus's Daughter (Mark 5:21-24; 35-43)	82
July 3—July 9 inclusive	Go Two by Two (Mark 6:7-13)	83
July 10—July 16 inclusive	David Dances (2 Samuel 6:1-19)	42
July 17—July 23 inclusive	N/A	
July 24—July 30 inclusive	A Boy's Lunch (John 6:1-15)	121
	Jesus Walks on Water (John 6:16-25)	122
July 31—August 6 inclusive	N/A	
August 7—August 13 inclusive	N/A	
August 14—August 20 inclusive	Solomon Becomes King (1 Kings 2:1-4; 3:1-15)	44
August 21—August 27 inclusive	Solomon Dedicates the Temple (1 Kings 8:1-66)	46
August 28—September 3 inclusive	N/A	
September 4—September 10 inclusive	N/A	
September 11—September 17 inclusive	N/A	
September18—September 24 inclusive	N/A	
September 25—October 1 inclusive	Courageous Queen (Esther 1–10)	52
October 2—October 8 inclusive	N/A	
October 9—October 15 inclusive	N/A	
October 16—October 22 inclusive	N/A	
October 23—October 29 inclusive	Bartimaeus Shouts to Jesus (Mark 10:46-52)	84
October 30—November 5 inclusive	Goodness (Ruth 1–4)	33
All Saints Day	N/A	
November 6—November 12 inclusive	Goodness (Ruth 1–4)	33
November 13—November 19 inclusive	Hannah Prays (1 Samuel 1:1-28)	34
Christ the King	N/A	
Thanksgiving Day	The Birds of the Air (Matthew 6:25-34)	68

Year C